# Philosophy

## *The Quest for Truth and Meaning*

### Andrew Beards

**A Michael Glazier Book**

## LITURGICAL PRESS

Collegeville, Minnesota

www.litpress.org

A Michael Glazier Book published by Liturgical Press.

Cover design by David Manahan, OSB. Detail of *The School of Athens*, a fresco by Raphael Sanzio, located in the Vatican.

1      2      3      4      5      6      7      8

**Library of Congress Cataloging-in-Publication Data**

Beards, Andrew.
    Philosophy : the quest for truth and meaning / Andrew Beards.
       p.    cm.
    "A Michael Glazier book."
    Includes index.
    ISBN 978-0-8146-5474-3 — ISBN 978-0-8146-5727-0 (e-book)
    1. Philosophy—Introductions.   I. Title.
  BD21.B325   2010
  100—dc22                                                   2009045526

# Contents

# Preface

This book aims to invite you into the world of philosophical reflection. There are a good number of introductory works on philosophy that, like this book, attempt to provide a user-friendly guide to the subject, so what is different about this one?

Many books introducing philosophy will rightly emphasize that in studying philosophy you will not be learning new material in the way you might learn new facts about the dark side of the moon. Rather, regarding many issues discussed you will be coming to know and have insight into things of which you have been in some sense aware for some time: things about yourself, about others around you, and about the world as a whole. This introduction stresses this aspect of philosophy since it is inspired by the thought of Bernard Lonergan (1904–84). Lonergan's thought is all about coming to discover in your own experience, to check out in your own consciousness the fundamental philosophical points he argues for. He does this in a consistent and thorough way, a way that, I believe, is found in few other thinkers.

The introduction to philosophy is, then, not primarily an introduction to Lonergan's thought but rather an introduction to philosophy inspired and influenced by his writing.

This book is addressed to anyone who wishes to reflect on the great realities of life, including those that have to do with human beings as persons who think, know, make choices, feel emotions, love, and seek answers to ultimate questions about the reason for their own existence and the meaning of it all. This book introduces you to some of the key areas of philosophy: the mind and its capacity to know truth and reality (cognitional structure and epistemology); fundamental structures and aspects of reality (metaphysics); the "good" and the "bad," the "right" and the "wrong" (ethics); and questions about the ultimate purpose of human life (philosophy of religion).

You will also notice in reading this book that the philosophical arguments and discussions in it sometimes make reference to the philosophical tradition of Catholic Christianity. This is in no way intended to restrict the readership of the book. On the contrary, the most recent popes have called for a renewed interest in and application of the resources of the great tradition of philosophical thinking within the Christian tradition. This is to enhance the dialogue and debate between believers and nonbelievers in society today by appealing to the common ground of our shared humanity: our shared ability to reason. In this way believers and nonbelievers may have a better chance of coming to agreement on vital social and ethical issues at stake in our modern world. Such a dialogue on the basis of reason may also allow unbelievers to better appreciate how the worldview of Christian believers is not a negation of human reason but, it may be argued, its fulfillment.

"*Philosophy: The Quest for Truth and Meaning* serves as an excellent textbook for those interested in the basic study of philosophy. Drawing inspiration from the writings of Bernard Lonergan, Andrew Beards guides his readers to reflect on the great realities of life and seek answers to the ultimate questions about the reason for their own existence and meaning by introducing them to some of the key areas of philosophy such as cognitional structure and epistemology, metaphysics, ethics, and philosophy of religion. Through its occasional references to the Catholic philosophical tradition, Beards also makes a sincere effort to enhance the dialogue and debate between believers and nonbelievers in society today by appealing to the common ground of our shared humanity: our shared ability to reason."

Robert Pen, SDB
Principal, Divyadaan
Salesian Institute of Philosophy
Don Bosco Marg
Nashik, India

"When I read *Method in Metaphysics*, by Andrew Beards, I was impressed with its clarity of prose and argumentation. Now, after having read *Philosophy: The Quest for Truth and Meaning*, I have proof that obscurity isn't the sole fate of philosophy. In his latest book, Beards takes us on a philosophical journey that is both illuminating and self-affirming. With deft subtlety, he discusses a breadth of philosophical topics ranging from reflections on the nature of philosophy itself to the existence of God. Importantly, he does this without leaving the reader awash in jargon that only a few can interpret. I highly recommend this book to those whose philosophical journeys are just starting, and especially to those who have been at it for a long time."

Lance Grigg, PhD
University of Lethbridge
Alberta, Canada

# Acknowledgments

Much of the material in this book has appeared in another form in course books produced for students on the Maryvale Institute's distance-learning BA in Philosophy and the Catholic Tradition. I would therefore like to thank Msgr. Paul Watson, director, and the International Maryvale Institute for permission to use this material in the book.

I also wish to express my gratitude to my wife Christina Beards for the invaluable help she has given me in correcting the errors in previous drafts of the work and in offering advice on ways to improve the text. Mr. Paul James, director of library services at the Maryvale Institute, compiled the index for this book. I am very grateful to him for his excellent work.

*Chapter 1*

# What Is This Thing Called "Philosophy"?

## The Great Questions

Throughout history and across human cultures we can see that human beings have raised and attempted to answer great questions such as the following: What is the meaning of it all? Why is there anything at all? Is death the end for us? Why is there suffering and evil in the world? What is the morally good way to live and to act? How can I know the truth? How can I find true love and happiness in life? That there are such questions, and the proposed answers, also reveals human beings as "the questioners," those who cannot help being oriented toward answers, answers about truth, goodness, love, meaning, and purpose. We begin to question when we are small children and keep going from there as we grow and learn more and more about ourselves, our community, and our world. This questioning is, then, wonder, and wonder, as the great philosopher Aristotle (d. 322 BC) said, is the beginning of philosophy.

Even when people's lives are full of the daily business of life, of getting through, these great questions have a habit of breaking into our lives. In moments of great joy and of great sorrow they appear on the horizon. When we mourn the death of a loved one the question about life's meaning comes up, and when we see the birth of a baby or see a beautiful mountain range at sunset the joy of the experience can also awaken our wonder at it all. These great questions are, of course, explored in the stories, myths, literature, poetry, and art of human cultures as well.

The great religions of the world also address these questions and offer answers. The difference is that philosophy raises these questions and attempts to offer answers to them using the resources of human intelligence and reason alone. Philosophy itself, however, may also discover the need to point beyond itself to religion: it may indicate ways in which the answers that a religion offers to the great questions of life are more comprehensive, complete, and satisfying than those that philosophy can offer alone.

The fact that such questioning and the desire for answers to live by arise spontaneously for us leads Pope John Paul II, in his great letter on the relationship between philosophy and religion *Fides et Ratio*, to claim that we are all philosophers by nature (4). Studying philosophy, then, is not like studying a particular science or a historical period we have not thought about before. It is the study of something much closer to home: it is the study of essential aspects of who we are and of what our world is. In many cases, as we shall see in the chapters to follow, it involves drawing out aspects of ourselves that in some obscure way we have been aware of for a long time. Once these aspects have been made an explicit theme for reflection then we can go on to see their consequences and understand ourselves, our human community, and our world in a more complete fashion.

## Stepping Back

In our world today people are familiar in all sorts of ways with taking time out, or stepping back from a busy life to reflect on that life or their activities in a more focused way. The idea of such withdrawal for reflection is that the renewed action that follows will be better in some way, will be enhanced. We see this when people go on training and staff development days and courses, when they go on retreats, when they meet with counselors of various kinds, even when they take a break to discuss things coming up in life or the world of work with friends or family.

Philosophy too can be understood as a "stepping back" in a similar fashion. The world of academic philosophy and the history of philosophy can be understood as the work of a community of human persons who pursue the great questions common to us all in a more sustained and concentrated manner. Naturally, the person of sound common sense will sometimes ask the relevance of all this. It can be a very good question. Often enough philosophers can seem to arrive at very meager results and go off into all kinds of trivialities. One might pick up a book on the philosophy of language, for example, and think after reading a page, "What has this got to do with the great questions of life?"

The view taken here is certainly not that all philosophy is equally good, sound, or satisfying. But the view in this book is that some of it is. On the other hand, it is true that what sometimes passes for common sense may not always be so; it may be common nonsense or even the bias and expression of the immoral attitudes of a particular culture and time. At some periods of human history the individuals who proposed to the majority that slavery is wrong may well have been told that their view was ridiculous, impractical, not of the "common sense" of the time. So common sense is not the ultimate arbiter of what is true and good.

Another point to make in this context is that the exploration of the great questions we have been thinking about can lead us off in all kinds of directions once we start investigating them. In a way this is how the various branches or fields of study in philosophy today can be seen as coming about and can, hopefully, be seen as being related.

Let us take the question "What is true love?" That seems to be one that has interested a lot of people, from the poets of all ages and times to the columnists of today's magazines, authors of popular novels, and hosts of TV shows.

We might start thinking of an answer in terms of the strength and duration of the passion and emotion shown between a man and a woman. But then someone might object: "Well, if it's only the strength of passions, what about the cases we read of when someone is obsessed with someone else, stalks them, threatens the life of the one pursued, or threatens suicide because of unrequited love? Or what about the domineering, possessive love of some parents for their children?" In fact this kind of discussion about human emotion and good or bad forms of human behavior is seen right at the beginning of Western philosophy in the dialogues of Socrates (d. 399 BC).

Socrates' dialogues are given to us filtered through the lens of the philosophy of his student Plato (d. 347 BC). In these dialogues or debates Plato shows us Socrates as engaged in debate with others in the ancient Athens of his time concerning the true nature of human moral qualities such as courage or the reverence one should show to one's parents. Just as we have seen in discussing the nature of true love, so also in the case of these Socratic discussions someone will bring forward an idea of what, for instance, true courage is, and objections will be raised. Socrates and his dialogue partners work in this fashion to try to get at a workable idea of what a human quality is or should be.

So, to return to our question about true love: The objector has said that true love can't be all about the sheer force of emotion or passion because we know of many cases when that leads to disastrous results for the very person said to be the object of love. Let's bring in Aristotle and St. Thomas Aquinas (d. 1274) at this point. Their contribution to the debate would be to say that true love has to involve "willing the good of the other." Now someone might respond to that by saying it sounds rather cold and unfeeling. But given the larger context in their works in which this idea is put forward, one would say that naturally this is not all Aristotle and Aquinas would say. Rather, what is involved in the true love between husband and wife will be different, both in terms of emotions and responsibilities, from the love between, say, parent and child. But, at the very least, they would claim, true love has to involve willing the good of the other, otherwise you will have all the problems of oppressing or manipulating the one said to be loved that you get when just powerful emotion is involved.

How does all this relate to the way one area of philosophy naturally leads into other areas? Well, in our discussion of true love the next question could very well be, "But what is willing the good of the other?" And here we run up against the question of ethics, of the nature of "right" and "wrong," of "good" and "bad." What is truly good for a human being? But things don't stop there, because that question will lead into the question, "What is a human being?"

If I come into my kitchen and find something is starting to burn in the frying pan, I may violently wave away the smoke. Is it morally wrong to violently wave away the smoke? We don't think so. But it might very well be wrong to do the same kind of action to my son when he is speaking to me, or even to the dog. Why? Because we take it that smoke, boys, and dogs are all very different kinds of being and that because they have the nature they have, that means it is right or wrong to treat them in this way or that.

Again you can see the way these questions were followed through in the story of the beginning of Western philosophy in ancient Greece. The great thing about Socrates is that he was a pursuer of the truth, and he knew some truth: that he *very often did not get to the truth* in the investigations he embarked on. But he knew that truth was a good thing and that we should seek it. When we come to Aristotle, however, we see that for him we have to produce a more detailed and developed plan than we see in Socrates' discussions. (To be fair, we may very well not know of all that Socrates wrote or produced.) So for Aristotle, if we are going to get an ethics, an account of dos and don'ts about what human beings should or should not do, we need to get a full-blown account of human nature. If we are trying to arrive at that, we need to compare and contrast human nature with all the natures of things we find around us in the world.

So it is that we see an account of what is right or wrong in behavior in Aristotle's philosophy, built on an analysis of human nature, and that analysis takes place in the context of a philosophical study of the human person's place in the world at large. Aristotle argues that by nature we humans are "rational animals." The philosophical investigation into the nature of the world and our place in it is what we call "metaphysics." Of course, today we might say, "Well, that was okay for ancient Greeks, but today we come to know the nature of the world through the sciences, through physics, biology, and chemistry," and someone might also add that as for human nature, we study this through human biology, psychology, and sociology. In fact, Aristotle did have quite a lot to say about the relationship between philosophy and physical science. He was a medical doctor and the son of a doctor, and he was fascinated by the physical world: he wrote about all kinds of things in the world, from animal biology to the nature of meteorites. We might want to say that some of what Aristotle wrote on the relationship between science and philosophy is no longer viable; on the other hand, we might argue that some of it is. But notice, this is precisely a philosophical question.

In fact, this only helps to lead us further in our outlining of the different areas of philosophy. So our questions about the relationship between philosophy and science are discussed in areas such as "philosophy of science." Some people have thought that with the coming of the modern sciences philosophy should really close up shop. But this has not happened, and indeed, as we shall see in the chapters to follow, it could not. *In fact, that view is itself not a scientific one but a philosophical one.*

So let us notice: our question about the nature of true love, a question that fascinates columnists in popular magazines, has already led us through ethics to questions about human nature and the world (metaphysics) to philosophy of science (how what the sciences say about human beings is related to what philosophy might say).

"But how can we know any of this?" might ask the skeptic. "Maybe you have all got it wrong, the scientists as much as the philosophers." Now, the question of how we know we "get it right" and how we know we "get it wrong" in coming to know the truth about reality is a question treated in .philosophy of cognition and epistemology. We are going to devote a good deal of space to these areas in this book. There are many other areas of philosophy in addition to the ones we have mentioned so far. For example, there is philosophy of art, or aesthetics; the study of logic, which is the study of our patterns of reasoning; the philosophy of history; political philosophy; and the list goes on. In each area a "philosophy of . . ." attempts to take that step back and look at an area of life in a sustained reflective and analytical manner, bringing to bear the resources of the rest of philosophy in doing so.

## A Conversation across Time

G. K. Chesterton (d. 1936) once remarked: "The only alternative to being influenced by thought-out thought is being influenced by un-thought-out thought." What he was getting at was that there is a danger in just drifting through life assuming all the views around us are correct. As we know from history, this can be a very dangerous road to follow: people can apathetically drift into all kinds of evil political and social compromises. The three great philosophers we have already mentioned—Socrates, Plato, and Aristotle—lived through a period of cultural upheaval and change, and this was the background for much of their truth seeking: once the assumed customs and ways of thinking of a culture are challenged, the question arises as to where and how we find ways of deciding what is true or false, good or bad. It is the existentialist thinkers of the recent philosophical past who have warned us against "inauthentically" fleeing from our nature as seekers of the true and the good, into the drifting crowd of modern society.

Philosophy, then, in its "stepping back" can help us gain something of a "critical distance" from our immediate culture. The philosopher William James (d. 1910) once remarked that "when most people say they are thinking they are merely reshuffling their prejudices." We might justifiably think this witticism overly cynical. But it has a point that we can see in our contemporary cultural setting. "Political correctness" is fast becoming a term of abuse in the contemporary West. Why? Because people sense that such "correctness" can sometimes be a set of moral rules that are just imposed by some kind of social authority in a way that denies critical assessment of just how justified these moral stances are in themselves. The assertion of such a worldview seems to be a matter of saying, "Well, that's just how things are and how we should be doing things in society," which blocks questioning and reasoned argument. It is no wonder that another of Chesterton's wonderfully ironic observations on modern society was that there are only two kinds of people: those who believe in dogmas and know that they do, and those who believe in dogmas and don't know that they do.

Take, for example, the relativistic views on truth and morality that are passed around in our culture as the views that any decent person, respecting a pluralistic worldview, should hold: "any view is as good/true as another";

"it's a matter of whatever feels right for you or your group." Far from being excitingly "new," such subjectivism and relativism are found at the very origins of Western philosophy in the thought of Sophists such as Protagoras and Gorgias in the fourth century BC. It was against such views that Socrates, Plato, and Aristotle offered their brilliant reflections on knowledge, morality, and human life, and some of the arguments they deployed against such skepticism are still relevant to our modern predicament.

The very study of the history of philosophy serves to take the sheen of "novelty" off such views: the fact is they have been proposed long ago. This is one of the liberating aspects of studying philosophy. Many introductions to philosophy mention the remark (intended as a thought-provoking exaggeration) of the twentieth-century philosopher Alfred North Whitehead (d. 1947): "All philosophy is just footnotes to Plato." It is an important lesson to learn that some of the most basic questions about human beings keep recurring throughout history, and we can profitably look back in order to go forward. Philosophers today are still wrestling with Aristotle's arguments as if he were a contemporary in debate, not simply a dead voice from the past. The point made in ancient times against such relativism can still be grasped by any intelligent human being today: to say that every view is as true as another is to put forward nonsense; for it is to exclude as false the view that would deny the truth of the view being put forward (that is, the view that holds "not every view is true, or as good as another"). In other words, if you hold A as true you automatically exclude not-A as false. You cannot have it both ways.

The fact that philosophy is a conversation with thinkers across time is itself a great philosophical lesson: it witnesses to the profound common humanity that we share with those who lived before us.

From among the many views of life offered to us in the busy marketplace of the mass media and world of communications, which are we going to accept? There is "no exit," as the French existentialist philosopher Jean-Paul Sartre (d. 1980) reminds us: for to choose none is still to choose. The resources of philosophy may be very helpful in making such decisive decisions about your life.

*Chapter 2*

# The Process of Coming to Know

## Introduction

Clearly, truth is a vital issue. One of John Henry Newman's (d. 1890) maxims was the Latin phrase *ex umbris et imaginibus in veritatem* ("out of darkness and fantasy into truth"). But in our contemporary Western culture we often meet the reaction that is akin to Pilate's reaction to Christ: "What is truth?" (John 18:38). Now, Pilate is in some ways a not unsympathetic figure for us. Perhaps we can see ourselves in him more than we can in, say, an out-and-out sadist or, indeed, in a saint. He is a cool, shrewd man of practical intelligence. He knows how to get on and advance in the whirligig world of Roman imperial politics and on the roller coaster of the political realities that were the Roman occupation of first-century Palestine. We sense from the gospel accounts that he was a man not devoid of all feeling. We know also, however, that he was a man who was prepared to cooperate in the death and destruction of the innocent.

This is a lesson for us today. Does the "cool," sophisticated, and apparently humane stance of the educated Westerners today who respond with indifference and skepticism to claims of objective truth, as Pilate did, not mask an apathy, a self-seeking indifference to anything beyond a nod of agreement to newspaper editorials that announce we should do more for the poor of the world or stop wars? If push comes to shove and the warm cocoon of Western consumer lifestyle were to be under pressure or were even to rupture, then is there not a fear that such a Western attitude of "freedom from any truth claim" could very easily descend openly into what the Marxist philosopher Herbert Marcuse (d. 1979) called "the tyranny of tolerance," that is, the position that since any view is as good as any other we will opt for the naked use of power in order to defend our comfort zone? Indeed, on a number of moral issues there are those who would say the West has already gone down this route, and this has in some way been linked to the idea of allowing all opinions as equal.

In Pope John Paul II's writing this is why the themes of *Fides et Ratio* are so intimately connected to his teaching on the foundations of morality in the encyclical of 1994, *Veritatis Splendor*. In Pope John Paul II's view, a legitimate plurality of views in democracy does not entail that a democracy can be built on a denial of any general moral truths, since this would be suicide for democracy. A true democracy must be based on moral absolutes that are the inviolable rights of individual persons in community; otherwise democracy can and will degenerate into the kind of mob rule that was seen in Nazi Germany, where the powerful and/or the more numerous simply vote for or decide for ethnic cleansing or persecution of the minority.

The question of truth, then, and our ability to know the objective truth about our world and ourselves, immediately opens out on the ethical, on questions of the good and bad, right and wrong, and how we should live as human persons.

People of our time often think that relativism about truth and the moral judgments of right and wrong have only recently been called into question by our discovery of other cultures that have very different views of the world and of morality from our own. But a study of philosophy can help liberate us from this current cultural illusion. Skepticism and relativism about truth stand at the very beginning of philosophy in the West. It was to respond to philosophers like the Sophists of ancient Greece who held such views that Socrates, Plato, and Aristotle expounded and argued for their views on human knowing. Later, St. Augustine (d. 430) also argued against skeptics of the Roman period after his conversion to the Catholic faith. And the knowledge of such views on skepticism and relativism is always there among philosophers, including those of the Middle Ages like St. Thomas Aquinas. It is, in fact, simple ignorance of this long history that leads some of our contemporaries to think that skepticism and relativism about objective truth are in some way the "discovery of modern man" and therefore only now have we arrived. But arrived at what? The truth? But is that not what we said we could not have?

Such questions bring us to a feature of the positions argued for in this book. Since the time of Socrates philosophers have pointed to the incoherence or the self-destructive nature of skeptical and relativistic arguments, and some philosophers have developed these counterarguments to skepticism in great detail. We will look at these in the chapters to follow. But here is one example to think about. We just spoke of a certain kind of relativism that holds that because we now know about all kinds of other cultures that hold different views of truth and morality, we cannot say there is any definite truth. But the position is incoherent, self-destructive in a number of ways. One is that it is based on claims to know truly all kinds of things about other cultures and their beliefs and to know these are different from mine. So I am claiming to know all these things about reality as a basis for my very argument. Or take one of those confused assertions someone might make in a discussion on these issues today: "Well, this is my 'own truth,' but it is not true for someone else." Again this is claiming to know what is true in general. For one thing, it claims to know that there is a "me" and a "you," and so on and so forth. Even when people talk of "mere opinion" similar confusions can enter into the discussion: "This is just my opinion," someone says. Yes, all right, but is it a good opinion? Are there reasons for holding it? What are they? If there are reasons for holding it, then okay, I am saying I am some way from definite truth, but I am still claiming this is probably true of reality with the degree of probability attached to the reasons given. If someone says, "It's just my opinion that there is a green elephant sitting on the breakfast table," and says they are not joking, then, despite their great modesty in saying, "but it's only my opinion, you know," we will still think the opinion is rubbish, even if charity forbids us from saying so.

The Pontius Pilate option of saying, "Well, we cannot get to objective truth," is not the only one in culture and philosophy that would oppose claims such as those made by Christians to a truth that comes from God. Other important and influential views on the theory of knowledge, or epistemology as it is called, would also challenge this position. "Empiricism," for instance, would say that truth can be known, but the truth we know is just a matter of seeing what is there to be seen, of touching what is there to be felt, tasting tastes, and hearing sounds. Therefore, to think that there is something like God who is beyond this world of sensations, who communicates truth to us, is to be involved in an illusion.

As we will see in what follows, it is very often the ding-dong battle between this empiricism, which says knowing is just seeing or the like, and its detractors that opens up the way for the Pilate-like cynics who say, "Well, it looks like we cannot get to truth anyway." We will need not only to examine how that and similar views are self-destructive but also to see that through a positive understanding of how we come to know objective truth about reality, we can show up the deficiencies of empiricist notions that hold that knowing the world is just a matter of seeing or tasting or touching or smelling or hearing the data that those senses detect.

## Making Explicit the Implicit

A way of introducing the study of epistemology, or human knowing, is to look at the question someone might put to us on this: "Why not study human knowing from the viewpoint of the sciences, like psychology or physics or biology?" In answer one can point out that when we consider examining human knowing simply and solely from the viewpoint of any of the sciences as they are understood today, we come to realize that such sciences presuppose the operations and criteria used in our human knowing: in other words, we *presuppose* the validity of our knowing operations when we say that these sciences do tell us something about the real world. Those sciences themselves, be they chemistry, physics, or psychology, do not reflect directly on the criteria operating in the human knowing that produced them as results.

To give an example: in logic there is a principle termed "noncontradiction." This is a rather high-sounding expression for something we have been aware of since we were quite small children. The principle states that something cannot be both true and false at the same time; so A and not-A cannot be true simultaneously. It is a principle studied in philosophical logic, and philosophers of logic express it in different ways in symbols and play about with it in all sorts of interesting ways (interesting, that is, if you are a philosopher of logic). But as I say, it is a principle that, while we never unpacked it in such big words when we were children, we were nevertheless aware of. When a four-year-old who is told there is milk in the fridge goes to have a look and sees none, he is aware that the statement "There is milk in the fridge" is false; it cannot be both true that there is some left in the jug and not true. As we shall see further below, what philosophy is often concerned with is to *make explicit what has always been implicit in our thinking and acting*. And St. Thomas Aquinas talks of such principles as being *per se nota*, or "naturally known" to us from childhood on. But returning to our point about science presupposing the validity of the knowing procedures that establish it, and not being directly concerned with those procedures, we can observe that this principle of noncontradiction is something a scientist can neither establish nor prove to be false by looking down a microscope.

Rather, all scientific argument and progress presupposes the principle. For we can characterize science as the attempt to verify a hypothesis on the basis of instances thought to be evidence for it. And when we verify some hypothesis as probably so, or true, then we may be ruling out as false some older hypothesis. If the modern theory of oxygen is true, then the older theories of air as phlogisten, or one of the four Greek elements, are false: it cannot be that both A and not-A are true.

If the various sciences, then, do not directly concern was and help us come to understand the procedures of our own knowing, what would the sort of philosophical reflection needed for the job look like? Well, in fact, we have been giving samples of it in the last couple of paragraphs. We have been noting some of the basic procedures that go on in science and some of the basic rational and logical principles that operate, and we noted that such principles, such as noncontradiction, are operative in our thought, whether as small children or as Einsteins, and that we use and operate with such principles without directly reflecting on them. But, as we shall see further below, it is very important not to fall into the confusion of saying that we therefore operate according to these principles unconsciously. The philosophical task will then be, in part, to make explicit what we have been doing implicitly. And this, when we are attempting to give an account of human knowing and, indeed, of other human activities, such as deciding and choosing, can be a quite fruitful way of proceeding. For, as we shall see, if the claim is made for an account of our knowing that this is what we have been doing in some way all along, but without explicitly identifying it, it should be possible to check out the proposed account of our knowing in our very own experience. Hopefully, we can move beyond a fruitless philosophical speculation on what knowing and its procedures might possibly be to an account that can be checked and verified in my own conscious experience, rather in the way that a scientist checks and verifies a theory against the data detected by his apparatus, his telescope or electron microscope.

## Consciousness

One of the phrases that comes to us from nineteenth- and twentieth-century literature is "stream of consciousness." The modern novel and other forms of art, such as poetry and theater, have manifested a fascination with the lived experience of consciousness in all its variegated hues and textures. One can think of examples such as Marcel Proust's *À La Recherche Du Temps Perdu* or, in an extreme form, James Joyce's *Finnegans Wake*. This interest has been conditioned by, and has itself conditioned, various styles of depth psychology, and historically the cultural role of philosophy has not been absent in these developments.

To begin our investigation into the process of coming to know, we can make two initial observations that the work of novelists, poets, psychiatrists, and others bring to our attention. First, we are not simply and solely knowing beings: if there are "elements of a process of knowing" that we are able to identify within our conscious experience and even if these elements have, as we shall argue, a definite structure to them, still that structure operates within the ebb and flow of conscious feelings, thoughts, and memories. Think of times you have stood staring out of a window, half looking at the scene, musing on, perhaps, different matters. The flow of consciousness may, in such cases, be very difficult to map out clearly.

It is the case, however, that whereas many of our waking states involve the buzz of many different "voices" in consciousness, still we may move or slip into certain patterns of experience where particular demands and aims are dominant and to the fore. We start the lecture off determined to pay attention and work at what is being said. Eventually, sometimes sooner rather than later, we start to drift. The great artist or scientist or mystic is one who has acquired the habitual capacity to pay attention to the work in hand and block out distractions. Indeed, it is our capacity to fall under the spell of wonder and ask, "Why?" which Aristotle identifies as the beginning of all philosophy. In identifying a structure of coming to know as present in my own experience, then, I will be isolating operations that occur alongside and in the midst of other elements in conscious experience or that, on some occasions, pretty much have the field if I am in a state where I am striving, or even moving with easy pleasure, to think something through.

Second, in writing about a stream of consciousness and the elements in it, novelists, poets, psychiatrists, and others are performing an activity that we noted above: the activity of attempting to *make what is implicit explicit*. When we read such works of poetry or novels what may impress us is precisely their power of saying something that we have often felt but were never able to articulate or put a name to. We may say, "Yes, that's it," on reading something that really strikes home in this way. What we want to do in the case of an account of our own knowing is, then, to express and articulate elements of a structure in consciousness in a rather similar way. What we are doing is not describing the dark side of the moon or a distant galaxy, but a state of affairs with which we have, in a strange but true sense, always been familiar but that we have never clearly articulated or come face-to-face with in an explicit way.

We have been talking of the stream of consciousness and of conscious experience. To get down to the business of outlining the structure of our knowing, we can begin by looking at the notion of consciousness itself, particularly as it regards this structure. Together with consciousness we will also discuss a closely allied notion: *intentionality*. And first we can note that all our knowing activities, the principle ones among which we are going to examine below, are *at once conscious and intentional*. By this we mean:

- conscious = aware
- intentional = "about" something

To say that "consciousness" means "awareness" is, as you may have noticed, not to have said anything very original: they are synonyms. But the point is really to help you catch on, via the use of various expressions, to a very basic experience. Another way to help you catch on or have an insight into what we are on to is to ask you to contrast being conscious with not being conscious of something. Be careful not to think of the immediate contrast to consciousness as *unconsciousness* as we tend to use that word conditioned as we are by certain styles of depth psychology (we need to get straight on that terminology a little later on). All we mean here is the blanket contrast between being conscious or aware of something and not being so. So I am conscious or aware in reading this of looking at marks on a page, but I am not conscious or aware of the circulation of the blood in my legs, unless I have some, perhaps unfortunate, medical complaint. And I am not conscious or aware of what is going on on a planet in the next galaxy (unless I am in contact with the requisite scientific equipment or, more directly, with aliens). Nor am I aware, as I am aware of my own thoughts and feelings as I read this now, of the conscious thoughts and feelings of people in houses down the street (unless I am a psychic or a St. John Vianney or Padre Pio). Below we will look at the notion of "self-consciousness," at the different kinds or qualities of consciousness, when we look at the different acts or operations that make up the structure of our coming to know, and we will also look at "the unity of consciousness." But to catch on to the initial, basic meaning of *consciousness* that we are starting with, all we have to do is to notice the contrast between being conscious and not being conscious of something, between being aware of something and not being aware of it.

## Intentionality

All the activities or operations in the structure of our knowing, which we will discuss below, are conscious, and all are *intentional*; that is, they are all "about something," "tending toward something." There is an "about-ness" about them. So when I am talking about my friend my talking is not about itself but about him: it *intends* him, points to him. Similarly, when I am listening to music or looking at a view, my mental activity is focused not on itself but on the beautiful view, on the change of theme. The word *intentional*, as we know, most readily conjures up moral images: "Did she do that on purpose? Was it intentional?" And indeed, this is a further illustration of what we are writing of. For as moral beings we *intend* in our moral questions, decisions, and choices to come to know moral truth about right and wrong, and to do what is right or wrong in our choices. If you like, what we are doing here is extending this terminology from the moral sphere to all our intellectual activities. Not that all of them are directly moral as choices are, but just as choices intend good or evil, just as we do or pursue good or evil intentionally or on purpose, so, sometimes, do we pursue factual truth, or attend to music or scenery or noises, intentionally or purposefully.

## Cognitional Structure

The next step in coming to know our own knowing is an exercise in counting up to three. That is, knowing can be identified as consisting of a set of mental operations, intentional and conscious mental acts occurring on three basic but interrelated levels:

1. The level of *experience*
2. The level of *understanding*
3. The level of *judgment*

Let us look at each level in turn.

### 1. The Level of Experience

This is the level on which we *see, hear, smell, touch, and taste* and have experiences of inner balance and the like. It is the level of sensate or sensible experience. And in the vast majority of cases our knowing begins with our *attending* to the *data* provided by our five senses. A mother needs to attend to the data provided by her toddler's red cheeks and reactions to things going into the mouth to conclude that her daughter has teething pains; a mechanic attends to the data provided by, among other things, the sound of the revved up engine to diagnose the problem; the scientist attends to the sights and sounds provided by his instruments in investigation (the sight of the changing color in the test tube or the moving needle on the dial); the historian must attend to the data of the ancient documents or the marks on stone if she is to pursue her investigation. Without our five senses we cannot imagine our knowing getting going. We know how incredibly skilled and creative people become in the face of the challenges presented by severe handicaps affecting the five senses. One thinks of the story of how Helen Keller overcame all the odds in this regard, but even she had to have the sense of touch.

One can see, then, how essential to knowing sensate experience is. The imagining and picturing we do in our minds is dependent on this. And there is an intimate connection between our sensations and the pictures and mental images that arise from them on the one hand and our human knowing on the other. In one of Plato's dialogues, the *Meno*, Plato has the story of Socrates and his friends discussing the nature of knowledge. At one point in the story Socrates has an uneducated slave boy come and join the company, and he asks the boy to work out a piece of Euclidean geometry by drawing diagrams in the dust. The boy fiddles about a bit with drawing the images in the dust and then, hey presto, he gets the insight and solves the puzzle.

The moral Plato draws from this is that this uneducated boy must have gotten the "know how" from somewhere to solve the puzzle, so his mind must have had a life before birth where this knowledge was imparted to him. And so we are off on the Platonic vision of the ideal forms of things as somehow seen by souls before birth. Aristotle, and Aquinas following him, however, would not see the story in that light. They would draw a different moral. For them what was crucial was the boy's fiddling about in the dust in order to get the insight. St. Thomas calls it "disposing the phantasm," or getting the images into such a constellation that the right answer just seems to leap out at you. But for Aristotle and Aquinas the story shows precisely the way human knowledge is intimately linked to the data of the five senses and the mental images and pictures that arise from this. Given this, St. Thomas argues that, simply in terms of philosophy, the idea of resurrection makes sense. For our knowing capacities are so dependent on sensation that although the soul can exist in a "diminished" state alone, it naturally requires the body for a state of existence proper to the fulfilled human being. Human knowing is not divine knowing and it is not angelic knowing.

Having said all this, it is certainly not the case that Aristotle and Aquinas are empiricists. *Empiricism* is the view that knowledge is simply and solely, or little more than, a matter of sensation: of seeing, smelling, hearing, tasting, and the like. Aquinas held that *"Nihil est in intellectu quod non prius fuerit in sensu"* ("There is nothing in the intellect which is not first in the senses," *De veritate*, q. 2, a. 3, arg. 19), indicating this intimate bond between our sensation, mental images, and our knowing. But the point is that the intellect itself is, for Aquinas, certainly not an empty box waiting to be filled; it is rather more like an empty stomach. That is, it has its own principles of operation and dynamisms with which it works on what it receives at the same time as being worked on itself. The error of empiricism is, then, to take it that knowing is solely an activity of just seeing, or the operation of any one sense. It is, rather, the combination of various intellectual activities on all three levels. As Lonergan puts it, the myth of empiricism is based on the error of mistaking what is obvious in knowing (we all know it does involve seeing and other sensate experiences) for what knowing obviously is. Sensation is essential to human knowing, but it is only one aspect. To see how it needs complementing we must move on to the next two levels.

## 2. The Level of Understanding

This level is characterized by such mental activities as *questioning, imagining, having insights, expressing insights in concepts, surmising, formulating hypotheses, theorizing*, and the like.

You hear a crash down the corridor and you spontaneously ask, "What is going on?" You see an odd expression on your friend's face in the morning and you think to yourself, "What's up?" The scientist looks at traces on a plate and asks, "What does that mean?" as does the scholar or the literary critic when she reads the page of a book, or the archaeologist when he finds some strange artifact on an archaeological dig. The first kind of activity we have mentioned in our list characterizing the level of understanding is the activity of *question, wonder*. It moves us from simple sensation to a wholly new flow of conscious activity. Now we are not looking at the data as would be someone in a drunken stupor, dumbly staring at it; rather the data of sensation is attended to with a question in mind. We are in an active, inquiring state with regard to it. Of course we want to get at the truth, at reality about our friend's mood, about what happened in ancient history, or what the nature of black holes is, but in human inquiry we have to go step-by-step: we cannot check out a hunch or a thought or an explanation until we have thought one up. That is precisely what this second level of activity, of understanding, is all about.

When we are trying to puzzle something out regarding, say, how to solve a crossword puzzle, what this theologian means in his book, why our friend was upset, or whatever, we are after an *insight*: a little act that we hope will make all the pieces fit together. This happens in all walks of life, as we have been suggesting. Human intelligence does not just suddenly kick in when one is doing something "academic." When we want some work done on our house or car, we go to the professional in whom insight is not a rare occurrence; we are not just interested in someone who has excellent seeing or hearing. But if we think of science or the courtroom, what we are talking about on this level is what is talked of in science as the "hypothesis" or in the courtroom as "the case for the defense" or "the case for the prosecution." The crucial point here is that there is something beyond this level in human knowing. For as Lonergan puts it, "insights are a dime a dozen." That is, even after we have hit on our insight, worked up our hypothesis, expressed our surmise or hunch about the reason for our friend's mood, there is still a further question to be met: is my surmise, hypothesis, idea, true to reality? For however brilliant or intricate the idea is, that does not necessarily imply it is true of reality. Think of all the interesting scientific hypotheses of the past or theories of history that have been abandoned. We can still understand these theories just as we can still understand a thought we had about our friend that turned out to be false. But understanding is not enough to give us knowledge of reality. We need judgment. We need to *attend* to the data if our inquiries are to get going, and we need to be as *intelligent* as we can in thinking up hypotheses to explain the data, but if we leave out judgment in assessing how likely our hypotheses are to be true of reality we are quite literally being unreasonable or rash. We need also to be *reasonable*.

Before going on to discuss the level of judgment, we can perhaps draw attention to a somewhat subtle distinction among the acts listed on the level of *understanding*. We do not want to dwell on this distinction too much, as you are being introduced to a lot of difficult new material, and it is best not to overcomplicate things. The distinction is between *insight* and *conception*. What we must first say is that both of these acts, just as all the other acts in cognitional structure, are conscious: we can check out that we do have experience of them by noticing what goes on in our conscious life. Nevertheless, we not only have the experience of consciously having insights but also of not trying, or trying but failing, or trying and succeeding in expressing our insights in words or concepts. That insights and concepts, or verbal packaging, are not the same can be seen from the way we can express the same insight in different verbal or even nonverbal ways. A good teacher knows the experience of having to communicate the same insight differently to different students. We also have the experience of not always expressing our insights in concepts or words as we want. We all know the experience of trying to put into words an answer to the teacher's question in class, only to feel the frustration of not expressing it as we want. Then some whiz kid gives the answer and we say to ourselves, "Yes, that's what I meant." The distinction between insight and conception is helpful in thinking about art. The musician and artist have insights and express these in patterned sounds and colors, in movement, in dance. And we either catch on to the insights or we do not. When we do not, we say we just do not understand this picture or this piece of music. But expressing the meaning we grasp in the work of art in words is a difficult and tricky thing. Yet we can sometimes hear or read a piece of art or music appreciation and say, "Yes, that's it, that's what that music meant to me." Notice we are not unconscious of the insights into the music we have enjoyed, if by unconscious we mean totally unaware. We were aware, conscious of the meaning, otherwise the music would be meaningless to us, and we would not recognize the piece of music appreciation as a good expression (conceptual formulation) of what we have experienced.

I think this distinction is strikingly brought home if one has small children. I am afraid that for all his brilliance, Ludwig Wittgenstein (d. 1951) missed out here (he had no children). For Wittgenstein there are just words but no mental insights that inform them. When one has small children, however, one sees daily how from very early on there are insights occurring before the child has the linguistic capacity to formulate them in words. I remember our son Max, when about a year old, clearly had quite a complicated set of insights in mind as to how he wanted to arrange some chairs near where I was sitting in order to make a traffic pattern across them and my legs for his cars. His only way of communicating this was through cries of frustration and by the pulling and pushing of things until I had arranged them perfectly to his satisfaction.

Finally, before we look at the level of judgment, we can briefly note that just as the empiricist makes the mistake of concentrating on level 1 to the exclusion of the other levels in his account of knowing, so a whole family of philosophical positions, reacting against empiricism, slip up by stressing level 2 without noticing properly level 3 (judgment). So idealists, relativists, and subjectivists of various kinds rightly point out that knowledge is not a matter of sensation alone and that we form concepts regarding the data. St. Thomas knew this when he wrote that if I say the sun is only the size of a football it is not my senses that are mistaken. What my senses do is give me data. Mistakes can happen in how I use this data in my theorizing. But the philosophies that emphasize level 2 miss level 3 and so are stuck in an impasse: all I have is a load of data on which I have imposed my conceptual schemes, the thoughts and ideas of my view or my culture. I cannot get outside these to check and see if they fit with reality, so I am stuck with a kind of skepticism or agnosticism about reality. We have noted some of these views in our historical sketch in chapter 6. They are represented by Protagoras in ancient Greece and by David Hume (d. 1776), Immanuel Kant (d. 1804), and Georg Wilhelm Friedrich Hegel (d. 1831), and by some existentialists and social relativists in the modern period.

### 3. The Level of Judgment

Cognitional structure is simply the structure of me when I am attempting to come to know. It is a *dynamic* structure. Why do we say it is dynamic? Because it is something on the move: I have or, it could be said, I am (among other things) a *desire to know*, and in this desire to know, I am, as it were, self-driven to move from data of sensation to understanding to checking out whether my understanding gets at the truth. This desire to know, then, takes the form of two basic sorts of questions that move me through the levels of cognitional structure: *What?* questions and *Is it so?* questions. St. Thomas, following Aristotle, knew of these two basic types, which in Latin were termed *Quid sit?* and *An sit?* questions.

We are driven from mere experience of the data of our senses by the questions "What is this? What is going on?" to the second level of trying to have insights into understanding what the data is. Similarly, we are driven on from our insights and hunches and theories on level 2 by the question "Is this so? Is this theory, insight, hunch true to reality?" This is the sort of thing that happens endlessly in science and scholarship. On the level of judgment we can identify further conscious, intentional mental activities: *marshalling the evidence; weighing the evidence; judging whether something is so, not so, probably so or not so, or that we do not have sufficient evidence or information—we need further inquiries.*

We can usefully think of the courtroom again here, and think of ourselves as a court. Levels 1 and 2 have been in operation: we have heard the case for the prosecution and defense, we have seen various data (video tapes, exhibits, and so on), and now it is time for the verdict (judgment) of guilty or not guilty. We know that, as in a court, so with various types of investigation in life, a number of options are open to us. We can declare a mistrial or dismiss the case. Perhaps the investigation has been on the wrong track; there is just a lack of any evidence one way or the other. On the other hand, we may be in a stronger position; the evidence and arguments warrant some kind of judgment: yes or no. If all the evidence is in, we are in the position to make a certain judgment. Very many of our judgments, however, are not in that position. Often they are probable judgments—yes or no—on the basis of present evidence. *In a judgment we are saying that our insight or concept definitely does or does not correspond with reality, or that it probably does or does not correspond with reality.*

## The Dynamic Unity of Consciousness

We have been talking about the variety of acts involved in coming to know, occurring on three levels. But here we want to stress a *unity*. If you remember, at the beginning of the chapter we talked about these knowing acts as occurring within the wider context of the stream of consciousness of the individual, who is not only a knower but a doer, a symbolizer, a lover of others and, hopefully, of God. We must recall that wider context here. And we can add that *in coming to know my knowing I come to know myself.* For although my knowing capacities are not the whole story about me, still they are certainly a part and a very important part. These knowing acts are then my acts; they are me in action. But what about the "me," the "I"? Do we just have a lot of individual acts? Certainly not, for as we have seen, these acts form a structure that is an interrelated set of acts. And these acts all occur in one consciousness, that is "me." For I am conscious of attending to sensation, of having insights, asking questions, and trying to judge. It is not one "I" that senses, another "I" that understands, another "I" that judges. Rather these various acts are distinguished by me in the one consciousness that I am. My conscious judgment would be just a meaningless, bare yes or no with nothing attached if I were not also conscious of the insights I am judging, and the data concerning which those insights arose. But this is not simply a passive unity of consciousness either. Certainly, there are passive moments to it: I cannot do anything about the noises I hear or the pains I feel. But it is also a dynamic consciousness. I am the one who has to make myself, with more or less ease, be attentive to the data, try to be intelligent, try to be reasonable. The dynamism is my questioning aspect that we noted above when discussing the two basic types of questions that move us through the levels.

Consider the following scenario that brings out what we mean by the operation of these various levels in coming to know. Two friends are walking along a foggy street. They begin to observe some objects in the distance. One friend hypothesizes that it is a truck that has turned over on its side. The other friend disagrees, saying that it is a set of more familiar objects, a postbox near the side of a shop, and so on. They both agree that more evidence is needed. Such evidence is provided as they approach: further data becomes visible, and a cry for help is heard. The first hypothesis is confirmed. In this little story we can identify the operations of the three levels in cognitional structure. We start with the data (level 1). Attention is drawn to objects in the distance, and intelligence (level 2) seeks an answer to the question "What is that?" Various hypotheses spring to mind, some of which seem equally good. One desires, however, not simply to muse on entertaining or ingenious hypotheses but to get at the truth. So with regard to any one hypothesis, one asks, "Is it so?" (level 3). Is there any evidence to judge that this hypothesis, rather than any of its rivals, is the case? Finally, the sense data provide evidence, and one judges that hypothesis *x* is so.

### *Coming to Know Objective Reality, Being, or What There Is*

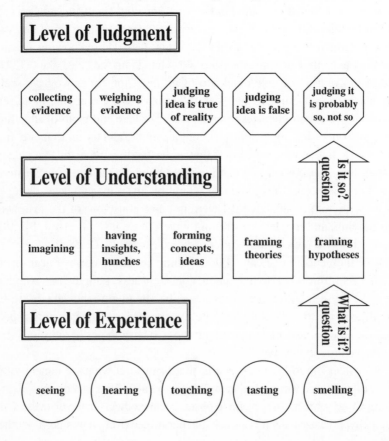

## The Boomerang Effect

In this section we concentrate on what the Lonergan scholar Terry Tekippe calls the "boomerang effect." This boomerang effect means that we use our minds to reflect on themselves and check out whether the account of cognitional structure we have been looking at fits the facts of our own mental experience. One of the first things to stress is that if we do find that the basic elements of cognitional structure are verified in our conscious experience, all we are saying is that these elements are at least truly the case. But that leaves open the possibility of ever further discoveries about our mental, intentional lives. This is true if we look at the history of philosophy. Aristotle's achievement in understanding the nature of mind and knowledge was further built on and developed by Aquinas. And the true elements in Augustine's theory of mind were also a contribution. There were, however, other theories of knowledge that from the beginning were more rather than less headed off track. Pretty much every philosopher's writings contains at least some truth. Part of this chapter will involve contrasting the view we have argued for here with some other views on knowledge. And a fruitful way of contrast is to note what in those views seems true and could be developed and what is ultimately inconsistent or *self-destructs when applied to itself.*

## From Self-Consciousness to Self-Knowledge

In order to understand our next move, verifying the account we have given of coming to know in our own consciousness, we need to reflect a little on the move from self-consciousness to self-knowledge. Because, as we shall argue, *we have been conscious of ourselves doing the knowing activities outlined on the three levels for years, but that does not mean that we have drawn up an explicit account of these acts and identified them as such before.*

Imagine that you are standing, looking out of the window, and a friend comes into the room. "A penny for your thoughts," he says. You reply, "Well, I was looking at the man with the wheelbarrow out there." Your friend says, "Yes, but you looked a bit worried too." "Yes," you say, "I was also thinking of poor Jim and his problems." "But weren't you thinking of the exam tomorrow?" inquires your friend. "Oh yes, that was on my mind as well," you answer.

What we can notice in this little exchange is the following:

- The thoughts and feelings going on in your mind when you were staring out of the window were all conscious. If they were unconscious, as unconscious as the flow of blood in your leg or the growth of your hair, you would not have been able gradually to relate them to your friend in response to his questions.

- But there is a difference between your being conscious of them and your identifying them in a report of what you were conscious of, drawn up in response to your friend's questions. Notice how tricky this process can be. Your conscious thoughts can be so bound up one with another in the flow of consciousness, they can be so fleeting that it is difficult to pin them down. But with the help of your friend's probings you do arrive at such a report. The *report* of your consciousness indicates what we mean by *self-knowledge*; the *conscious flow* prior to the report, on which the report is based, is *self-consciousness*.

But what do we mean by the "self" in self-consciousness? We saw above, when discussing intentionality, that all our conscious acts are about something: they may be about our friend's mood, about the tree we are looking at outside, about the color of this chair, about a problem in math or theology, about the love of God, and so on. And, thus, when we are attending to these things we are clearly *conscious of them*. But it is also true to say that we are at the same time *conscious of ourselves*.

This can sound rather odd at first glance, but really it is an obvious part of our experience. When my friend asks me what I am looking at out the window and what other things I am thinking about, I report not only "wheelbarrow," "Jim's sad state," and "exam tomorrow" but also "*I* am thinking about Jim," "*I* am enjoying the sight of the brightly colored wheelbarrow," "*I* am thinking nervously about the exam." I am not only conscious of the thing, but strangely, of *my being conscious* of the thing. Otherwise I could not include the information about *my conscious involvement* with these objects of my thought in my final report, drawn up with the help of my friend. This is further brought out if we reflect on the various ways or modes in which I may be consciously intending the various contents of my thought. So, I may be staring blankly at the wheelbarrow, or I may be enjoying its look aesthetically, or I may be asking a question about its state of repair. In these instances my conscious intending of the wheelbarrow will vary concerning the same object.

With regard to the move from self-consciousness to self-knowledge on my own cognitional structure this will also be the case. For some years already I have been aware of myself as consciously attending to data, consciously asking What? questions about it, consciously having insights, consciously asking if they are true, and consciously judging on the issue. But now I am moving from those conscious activities, in which I was conscious not only of the many things or issues about which I was thinking but also of my type of thinking about them, to a report, a self-knowledge account of that which I have been doing for years already.

The point is, then, that I need to check out, or verify, the cognitional structure that we have been outlining in the data of my own conscious activity. Remember that the theory of knowing itself said about me that I do not rest content with interesting theories but that I raise the further questions, "Is it so? Is it true to reality?" Now then, I am raising these questions with regard to the theory of knowing itself.

Before I invite you to perform the experiment of trying to verify in the data of your own conscious experience the theory of cognitional structure we have outlined, I will just dwell for a little on something very relevant to this testing, or verifying. It is a notorious fact that in the history of philosophy very many theories, when applied to themselves, *self-destruct*. The twentieth-century British philosopher F. P. Ramsey (d. 1930) gave a very good, simple example of what is meant here. Imagine a man who tells us, "I can never say the word 'marmalade' without stuttering it." But now imagine that he puts forth this sentence perfectly clearly without any word being stuttered over. What has happened is that his own performance has given the lie to the very sentence he was putting forward as true. His truth claim self-destructs in the act of making it. Perhaps he does not notice this at all. Maybe we record it on tape and play it back to him. Then he can say, "Yes, you're right, I have done it without stuttering." This, then, would be noticing in the data of his own experience that he has evidence for the judgment, "I can say 'marmalade' without stuttering."

In order to verify cognitional structure, then, we can note that the attempt to deny it will land us in a self-destructive position. To argue against cognitional structure we must use the structure, and we can notice we are using it by attending to our own conscious experience as we argue. So we cannot consistently judge that we make no judgments. We cannot consistently claim to know that we do not know. In disagreeing with the account of cognitional structure one would have to attend to the data on the matter, in this case the pages above or elsewhere where the account is outlined, and the data of one's own cognitive activities; one would have to understand what the account said in order to disagree with it; one would have to raise the question, "Is cognitional theory correct, partially correct, totally wrong?" in order to pursue one's disagreement with the theory and give some judgment on this. In other words, one would be in the position of arguing that one does not argue; one would be in the position of using cognitional structure to assess it.

This kind of argument, turning an argument back on itself to show that it must actually use what it is attempting to deny, has been known from the beginning of philosophy. What we are doing here is relating Lonergan's quite lengthy and developed form of such arguments in the area of knowing theory. But this kind of argument was used by Aristotle against the skeptic to show that the skeptic must use reasoning to deny it. Such arguments are found in St. Augustine, John Henry Newman, and many other philosophers. St. Thomas recognizes the force of this kind of argument when he acknowledges that the man who denies that there is any truth involves himself in incoherence, for he is claiming, "It is true (I know the truth) that there is no truth." Of course, you could just sing the words "there is no truth" or "I know nothing" for the aesthetic feel of the words, if one were a foreigner to English and did not understand their meaning. One only becomes involved in incoherence when one puts them forth as *truth-claims, as judgments.*

Here we are getting to the subtler point on what kind of incoherence is involved here and why we cannot reasonably deny cognitional structure without verifying it. And it is a point to do with the move from self-consciousness to self-knowledge—from one's thoughts to an explicit report of them. Just like the man who says in a smooth voice, "I cannot say 'marmalade' without stuttering," so the person who says, "I do not make judgments," (*if he intends these words as a judgment*) can be brought to revise that judgment as incorrect, or false, by attending to the data, or evidence, on the issue. In the case of the marmalade stutterer the data are the sounds in the air of the word "marmalade" (perhaps captured on a tape recorder). In the case of the person claiming "not to judge," the data to which their attention must turn is the data of their own consciousness, their own conscious act in putting forward those words about judging with the meaning they have. *That is, they must attend to the data that show that their own act is a conscious intentional act of judging, although this is what they are denying they do.*

## Knowledge of Reality, Being

What is the approach here to showing that our knowledge can be objective, that it can reach reality? Very simply, the answer has already been given in our previous sections on cognitional structure: we outlined a basic theory of coming to know, and then you were invited to verify whether that structure was true to the facts of your conscious experience. It was argued that you could verify the account as being really so, for in trying to deny it, or argue against it, you could notice that the very acts you were denying, the acts on the three levels, were really and truly going on in the very process of reasoning or arguing about the truth or falsity of cognitional structure. Knowing cognitional structure is an instance of knowing reality or objective knowing. For to see that I cannot judge that I do not judge, I need to notice that the act putting forward these words is really and truly a conscious act of judging going on in my experience.

In the eighteenth century, the German philosopher Immanuel Kant developed a form of idealism that stressed the manner in which our minds have all kinds of ways of categorizing the data of our experience, but that we do not know if our ideas or categories get at objective reality. We impose our categories on the "stuff" that comes in through our senses, but as to the real nature of that stuff we are in the dark. We can know things as they appear to us but not things in themselves. Hegel followed this path, as did and do many of the subjectivist philosophers of the modern period. Nevertheless, despite the profundity of much of this analysis, and the elements in it that remain of value, the final conclusion of Kant's and Hegel's thought ends up in the same kind of self-destructive situation as our marmalade stutterer. For what these positions ultimately boil down to is the claim, or judgment, *it is really so that I cannot know what is really so.* That is, I claim to know *really and truly* that human beings have such and such knowing capacities, that *really and truly* they have such and such limitations, and that *really and truly* their knowing does not hook onto a real world. I am claiming to know a great deal about reality while denying that I can do so. And if these are not claims to know objective reality, then we need not bother with them if that is what we are interested in knowing. By making such claims, as Kant and Hegel do, I am claiming to know as an objective fact that I am not God, that I do not know everything about everything. I am claiming to know my limitations, or that I only know appearance. But in so doing I am implicitly asserting that for these claims at least I am not lost in appearances, ignorant, or deprived of true knowledge through my limitations. To know a limitation as a limitation is to know an aspect of reality, what is, being.

Another way of thinking about this is to reflect on the problem of the so-called bridge. On this view, I am an "in-here" mind that cannot get through knowledge over the bridge and know a real "out-there" world. But in setting up the situation in this way I have already made a number of judgments about reality. That is, that the situation is really and truly as I describe it. Thus I have crossed the bridge to an objective knowledge of reality without even noticing it.

Part of the problem here is the persistent myth that "knowing is seeing." The empiricist and the naive realist think this, and it is understandable in a way that they do. Seeing is very obviously one element in coming to know. But as we have seen in cognitional structure, it is only one element. For St. Thomas Aquinas reality is known in judgment, not simply in sensation. So when the "knowing as looking" idea is challenged by the idealist, social relativist, or skeptic, we end up with the idea that all we have is our subjective ideas of the world and not knowledge of what is, of being. For they follow the myth of knowing as just seeing, as does the naive realist or the empiricist. The difference is that whereas the naive realist and empiricist just take it that our looking is a successful recording of reality, the idealist and skeptic say, "No, we cannot get out of our skins to get to a higher position and check that our looking really does get at what we suppose it looks at." But, this is myth. Knowing is not simply looking. Knowing involves the various activities we have looked at on the three levels and culminates in judgment. In judgment we claim that our ideas or concepts do or do not correspond with reality. And as we have seen above, the idealist, social relativist, or skeptic makes *judgments about what is really and truly the case concerning human knowing and its limitations as much as the next person.*

Let us notice how we are getting to reality, to objective knowledge, in refuting the Kantian or idealist positions. The Kantian says, "I cannot know reality, being, what is the case." How do we refute this? By getting him to attend to the data of his own consciousness. That is, we get him to attend to the fact that the very act he makes in putting forth his claim is a judgment that claims to know reality. *Thus, in order for the refutation to take place, in order for it to work, the Kantian must grasp that really and truly an act of a certain kind has occurred in his consciousness: an act of truth claiming, an act of judgment, of saying what is so. The refutation only works because it is based on an instance of coming to know objective reality: that is, the reality of this mental act of a certain kind.*

What about knowledge of other things apart from my mental acts? Well, we have seen that the various acts on the three levels of cognitional structure are really and truly the case, because even if we try to deny them we find the evidence for them in the data of our own consciousness as we argue or deny. Clearly, we are not in quite this situation with many of the other judgments in life, science, or scholarship. What is important to grasp is that we can see in the case of our mental acts, all the evidence is in for the judgment or verdict of the court. We cannot doubt the judgment without showing that this evidence is in. We do have in all the other areas of life, however, the same experience of being intelligent and reasonable in trying to come to judgments about reality. We may not be in the situation to say that all the evidence is in, but we can be in varying degrees of assessing that it is reasonable to assert $x$ and deny $y$ because more evidence is in for $x$, and we know that rules out $y$. What we mean here is probable judgments. We know from April Fools' Day tricks or the television programs that set up elaborate hoaxes for a laugh that we might be fooled in all sorts of apparently normal circumstances. So we cannot claim certainty here. We cannot claim that we know all the evidence is in. So I might come into my room, sure that when I touch this keyboard the usual things will happen. The computer will fire up or will misbehave in the expected fashion. But, the keyboard turns out to be a very clever hoax—perhaps a cardboard substitute.

In these areas, however, our judgments, probable judgments about reality, are reasonable insofar as we have some evidence. I have no reason to suspect a hoax; the look of the thing is normal, and so on. I might start to be suspicious if I have been involved in a round of such clever hoaxes with and against my friends and this is my birthday. But note, here again I am using my intelligence and reason to bring into consideration all the relevant factors helping me to assess the data. To conclude, if there is something here that looks and feels like a keyboard, or if there is something here that looks, feels, and smells like an onion, I have reason for the highly probable judgments that "this is a keyboard" or "this is an onion" in a way that I would have no reason to make those claims if what was before me looked like a birthday cake or a sports car. Yes, I could revise my judgment and find it was a clever hoax (the revision would be a further exercise of my intelligence and reason in coming to know), but insofar as I have evidence for the first set of judgments and not for the second set, I am being reasonable in making the probable judgments that I do. We will look a bit more at this issue when we have a brief look at science in our next chapter.

# Chapter 3

# Knowing in Common Sense, Science, History, and Art

## Knowing Is a Basic Activity in Human Life

In the previous chapter we have explored the three interrelated levels of conscious activity (experience, understanding, and judgment), which lead to objective knowledge of reality. That we can reach objective knowledge of reality has also been argued. We have seen that the attempt to deny objective knowledge lands in a self-destructive position. For we will be claiming to know true facts about reality, that is, about the reality that is our minds and their capacities and limitations. Further, we know such positions to be self-destructive and therefore false, because in trying to affirm them we find unavoidable evidence that there are realities that we can know. These are the realities that are the conscious acts on the three levels of coming to know. So, for instance, if I make the judgment, "I make no judgments," it is shown to be false by the conscious act of judging, which I engage in making the claim. Therefore, I know that claim is self-destructive and false. But I do so because I notice in my own conscious activity that a real conscious act of judgment has occurred. The knowledge of that reality, the conscious act of judgment, is what shows that the claim that "I make no judgments" is false.

The whole idea of trying to get from an "in-here" subjective mind to an "out-there" objective reality is, as we have seen, then, totally confused. For getting to know the reality that is my mind is getting to know a bit of reality, just as another part of reality is the number 19 bus. In getting to know either part of reality—the bus or my mind—I have to engage in the same activities: I have to be attentive to the data, as intelligent as I can in trying to understand the data (in gaining insight into the data), as reasonable as I can in assessing whether my understanding can be judged as corresponding with reality.

The whole point of the account of knowledge offered in this book is that it is claimed to be verifiable, checkable, at least in its basic, fundamental outlines, in your own conscious experience.

What you have encountered in this book so far is certainly difficult and demanding material. And it is demanding precisely because you will not get it, you will not get the insights or have the penny drop, without going over the material with reference to your own mental experience. You need to *appropriate* the material—make it your own.

In this chapter we will attempt to become more familiar with the account of knowing objective reality by examining ways in which this helps us understand human knowing in diverse spheres of activity: in common sense, science, history, and art. By examining these areas of human activity we will see that the account of knowing we have been studying helps us understand a basic unity between these various human activities and at the same time helps us to understand what is distinct about them.

## Common Sense

If coming to know reality is a matter of experience of data, understanding the data, and verifying in judgments the correctness of our understanding, then on occasion we may be required to make a personal effort to get to know something correctly. We have to be *attentive* to the data, we have to be *intelligent* in trying to understand the data, and we have to be *reasonable* in assessing in judgment whether our ideas correspond to reality. So already there is an element of willing, of moral effort, that enters into the process of coming to know. That we can also think of a fourth level or phase that is the level in consciousness of moral responsibility is something we will reflect on briefly below. The point I want to make here, however, is that, as has been stressed in the previous chapter, the process of coming to know that we have been studying is one with which we are all very familiar; it is a process we have been involved in since early childhood but that we have not explicitly reflected on (recall, we have not been unconscious of it—a crazy idea!—but we have not stopped to give a detailed report of it in self-knowledge). That we have all been involved in this process but have not been much concerned to give an account of it is witnessed to by the way we can all appreciate from our commonsense experience the point of the precepts given above: if you want to get correct knowledge, you must be attentive, try to exercise what God-given intelligence you have, and be reasonable in assessing the evidence. This is the kind of advice teachers and parents have been giving us by word and example for years.

If you are *inattentive* to the data, you will not get far in knowledge. If you are *silly* rather than trying to be intelligent in thinking up explanations for things, then you will not get far in knowing the world; if you are *rash* rather than reasonable, again this will not help you attain objective knowledge. If a judge finds his whole jury is made up of people who rush to conclusions, rush to a verdict of guilty or not guilty without having heard the relevant evidence, he will certainly want to find new jury members. If the jury members let emotions get in the way of a reasoned judgment ("she is a pretty girl," "he is so well spoken"—they cannot be guilty), they will be of no use in pursuing the course of justice in the court. In fact, this point shows us that what is at work in any given society is not only common sense but common nonsense, and there may be a confusing mixture of the two.

Clearly, all of us think that in making a sandwich we are employing the intelligent and reasonable operations that are part of common sense. But even in everyday small actions, wider issues are involved. So the man who is a vegetarian will want to use his intelligence and reason to look further in the freezer or fridge for ingredients to make his children a sandwich than the person who is happy to grab the first thing that comes to hand—some cold chicken. G. K. Chesterton remarked that a person's philosophy of life is the most practical thing about him or her. Thus we know very well that in the societies in which we live what passes as common sense we may wish to reject vehemently as common nonsense: "It is common sense for her to use contraception," we hear someone say; or, "It is only common sense for him to move in with his girlfriend"; or, "It is common sense to treat people from inferior countries as inferior to us." As a Catholic one would, or should, have a very different common sense, one that views such pieces of advice as morally damaging to the persons involved, advice that, in some fundamental way, is not the result of ethical positions arrived at through consistent application of attentiveness, intelligence, and reasonableness.

So we need to be aware that not everything we may refer to in our culture as common sense is in fact so. But given these important considerations, which again connect the account of knowing with the ethical area of philosophy, what we wish to focus on in the remaining treatment of common sense in this chapter is the way the conscious intelligent and reasonable processes occur in everyday understanding. This will help us when we consider the relationship between commonsense knowing and scientific knowing.

Unlike science, commonsense, or our ordinary understanding, does not aim to give explanatory knowledge of the things in the world around us, nor, therefore, does it aim to give explanatory definitions. As we saw in the previous chapter, in our daily lives we experience a flow or stream of consciousness. This stream of consciousness is that which novelists, psychiatrists, poets, and spiritual writers are concerned to describe and explore. The three phases or levels of coming to know are aspects of that daily flow of consciousness. We can now focus more on an intellectual problem, now on some aesthetic experience (I hear some beautiful music in a distant room), now on interpersonal feelings. All these elements are part of the tapestry of our daily flow of consciousness. Lonergan writes of this daily mixture of conscious patterns in the flow of consciousness as what characterizes the person as the "dramatic subject." And the German philosopher Martin Heidegger (d. 1976) speaks of "man dwelling poetically."

Thus our ordinary language expresses this complex flow of elements in our consciousness. Our ordinary language does not strain, as does mathematical language or scientific language, to be precise in its definitions. Rather, ordinary language expresses not only our intelligence and reasonableness, and our lack of these as we saw above, but also our emotional and aesthetic orientations. The words and phrases of such language when analyzed are often metaphors, pieces of poetry and the use of words and phrases that communicate insights in an elliptical and elusive way: "A nod is as good as a wink."

In fact, one philosophical program pursued by some English-speaking philosophers of language in the earlier part of the twentieth century ran aground precisely because of this great difference between the use of ordinary language and that of scientific language. Wittgenstein, in his earlier work, as expressed in his 1922 *Tractatus Logico-Philosophicus*, tried to map out the logic of a meaningful ordinary language as you would map out the logic of mathematical language. He later came to repudiate in a quite aggressive way his earlier naivete about ordinary language. The story goes that this was already underway in the 1920s, and one thing that helped him to see how mistaken it was happened during a conversation with an Italian philosopher who expressed some point with a typical Neapolitan gesture of the hand.

In fact, the account of human knowing we began to study in the last chapter is of considerable help in this context. As we shall see further when we reflect on knowing in art, insight helps us to understand the way we grasp meaning in an immediate way in gestures, facial expressions, poetical lines, and advertising. As we saw in the last chapter, we can have a very fleeting experience of insight into such data, and it may be difficult to conceptualize or verbalize in a complete way what we have understood. So if I am listening to a poem by W. H. Auden, it does have meaning for me as it would not for a three-year-old. I have some insights into it in a way that I do not have into an untranslated Chinese poem, since I speak no Chinese languages. But ask me to give an account in precise terms of what I have understood in Auden's poem, the message or messages he is getting across, the subtle evocations of feeling and image he achieves in his rhyme, and I may be hard put to give an adequate response. Perhaps with time, and with the help of some literary critical writing, I might get nearer to giving such a conceptual account of what I had grasped in insight.

Mathematical and scientific language, however, aims at definition that is precise. A scientist cannot be content with singing "The Moon's a Balloon" and leaving it at that. He or she strives toward explanatory knowledge: a knowledge of things related among themselves. In ordinary understanding we may be content to simply describe things as related to our purposes. This point was seen long ago by Aristotle, who said that the man experienced in giving the right herbal medicine knows to give such and such a plant in such and such circumstances. The doctor, on the other hand, is the one who knows, or who wants to know, *why* it is that this plant heals.

Again, common sense is happy to give out set pieces of advice and to make generalizations, but if we tried to put these together in some logical system, we would end up with contradictions. So we are told both that "the pen is mightier than the sword" and that "sticks and stones may break my bones, but words will never hurt me," and we are advised to "look before you leap" and that "he who hesitates is lost." Clearly, however, only a bore would object to these as not constituting a logical system. Common sense knows that they are to be applied in given circumstances when other insights and judgments have been made into the circumstances: only apply them when and if they are relevant.

Similarly, generalizations occur in common sense. People classify things by the way they appear and behave. But at some later stage science may wish to overturn such classifications in the name of explanatory knowledge: so whales turn out not to be fish but mammals. We need to understand, however, that in our contemporary culture there is also a two-way exchange between common sense and science. In fact, the exchange between the theoretical domains, like that of science and philosophy, and common sense has had a long history. So, ordinary language as contained in the dictionaries of modern Western languages will be found to have a long history in which cultural forces such as Greek and Roman culture and Christianity have had a profound effect. The increased success of science and the profound effect of technology on ordinary life have also affected our languages and the way we see ourselves and the world. Common sense inevitably has a pragmatic orientation from which its users judge the success of theoreticians. So while at one time it may have pooh-poohed the pretensions of scientists (see Swift's mockery of them in *Gulliver's Travels*), it then became enamored of science as it proved effective in transforming the environment of everyday life for the better. In recent years, however, we have seen something of what is perhaps a healthy distance grow between the public and the scientists, as the morally questionable products of science, nuclear power, genetic manipulation, and so on, are viewed with suspicion.

Such a suspicion witnesses to the healthy instincts operative in common sense as sensible. But as was outlined above, common sense can also degenerate into common nonsense, and one form this takes is the manifestation in common sense of a claim to omnicompetence: "what use is that theory to me?" This can be the common objection raised to some theoretical viewpoints. The problem here is that history shows societies in which a demanding, even self-sacrificing, moral viewpoint may be simply dismissed as unrealistic by the community, and some immoral, shortsighted viewpoint that seems more comfortable is endorsed. So, for example, if Hitler gets the trains running and does good things with youth groups and employment, we will overlook his violently racist philosophy.

These general considerations about common sense are, then, to our purpose, since they draw our attention to the way attentiveness to data, intelligence in thinking about how the data are to be understood, and judgment about the truth of that understanding may or may not be present in varying degrees in the lives of individuals and societies. In the previous chapter, examples given of the process of coming to know included very down-to-earth, ordinary instances. And here we can stress again that this process of coming to know is involved in ordinary tasks and interpersonal relationships. Seeing or sensing is part of knowledge but it is only part—an aspect of level 1: experience. When we take our car to the mechanic it is helpful that he has adequate vision. But we would rather choose a mechanic to fix the car who not only had adequate vision but also good mastery and familiarity through acquired insights and sound judgments into car mechanics than one who has superb vision but little know-how.

Our knowing experiences include the orientations we share with animals. So small babies reach for their mother's breast, but the phenomenon of human knowing includes distinctively human moments that, as far as we can judge, are not shared by the animals. Thus, we experience the three-leveled unfolding of the process of coming to know. But we should also bear in mind that we may not always be going through the process to judgment in a long drawn-out way. In acquiring new knowledge this may be the case. But the process can also happen very rapidly. The expert has acquired familiarity and mastery of a given situation, and so judgments on situations occur rapidly. On the first day in the factory everything is pretty bewildering. But after two years the know-how we have acquired makes what we do second nature, and we wonder that the newcomer can look so lost. The process of coming to know can therefore regard not only knowledge of facts about the world, about reality, but know-how, practical knowledge. At one time we needed to go through a process of trial and error, a self-correcting process of knowing, in order to learn how to tie our shoelaces, but now the actions happen with ease. We can note in passing that Aristotle and Aquinas stress the way such know-how is a habit. There can be practical habits (again, acquired via experience, understanding, and judgment), moral habits (the virtues and vices), and intellectual habits (the acquisition of the knowledge of some area like science or history). It is a characteristic of such habits, as Aristotle points out, that we experience difficulty in acquiring them, but once we have done so we perform acts with an ease and pleasure that shows we have the habit or capacity.

In all such learning the moment of insight, of "Yes, I've got it," which Lonergan analyzes, is key. A good teacher is one who can facilitate, elicit, or educe insights in his or her students. He or she has to find the right way of arranging the data so that the insights can occur for students.

## Commonsense Knowing and Scientific Knowing

One of the things studying philosophy teaches us is that very often we caricature the past from our own cultural viewpoint. If we actually study the past in, say, studying philosophy, we will be struck by both continuities and discontinuities in the area of human thinking. One myth about the philosophical past is that before the rise of modern science the ancients and medievals all thought they knew everything about the world; they had it all wrapped up, as it were. Now, as with all myths, this one has elements of truth to it. That is, there were philosophical viewpoints that pretty much held that nothing else of significance could be known apart from what was already known in some philosophical system, and such a viewpoint would seem to block the idea of growth in knowledge as occurs in science. Much more could be said in this area, but we do not want to reproduce here the whole philosophy of science. What can be pointed out for our purposes, as we study the area of human knowing, is that many of the ideas of the birth of science and its alleged replacements of philosophies such as Aristotelianism and the like, have been shown to be wide of the mark historically by twentieth-century scholars such as A. C. Crombie (d. 1996).

It would appear that decisive moments in the emergence of modern science occurred in the ancient Greek world, where we see the determination to investigate the world rationally; in the medieval Western world, with its theological beliefs about the rationality of creation and its attempts to engage in experimentation to see how the Creator had acted; and in the early modern period in which is witnessed institutional and communal efforts and commitments to create forms of experimental inquiry that were well supported technologically and socially.

With our knowledge of the history of science and its intimate relation to the history of philosophy, we can certainly say that some philosophies actively encouraged the scientific enterprise and were indeed its seedbed. Thus, St. Thomas Aquinas's doctrine that beings are composed of essence (a "what") and existence (a "that it is") in metaphysics did not entail that he thought he knew the important facts about the world in advance. Rather, he asserted that we know very little of the essences of the things in the world around us. In his *Commentary on St. John's Gospel*, Aquinas at one point remarks that he does not know the explanatory nature of a stone and that it would probably take a lot of investigation to find out just what the nature of a stone is. Clearly, there is the openness to scientific knowing and the virtual invitation to engage in it. In fact, near contemporaries of St. Thomas, like Theodoric of Freiberg (d. 1310), another Dominican, were engaged in experimental research. And Theodoric is known for his discovery of the nature (what we still take as the nature) of the primary and secondary rainbow.

In the Renaissance, we see the philosophical discussion regarding what were termed "primary" and "secondary" qualities coming to a head. Given the rapid development of the sciences in this period, and the use of new devices such as the telescope (from 1609) and microscope, the question arose about the relation between the thing that appears and its true, hidden nature inside. Aquinas's point about the essence of the stone is seen in this new determination to find out what the inner nature of the object is. But what of its outward appearance, then, the appearance that had always been known to common sense? Is the inner makeup of a red rose, known by science, the true thing, while the beautiful object known to common sense is some kind of illusion, like a mirage? Such were some of the issues for human knowing that seemed to become pressing as the development of the scientific enterprise went on and its achievements convinced an increasing number of people of its validity.

Such epistemological questions arising from science are still with us, and one extreme view, expressed during one phase of a career in which he changed his mind often, was that expressed by the twentieth-century philosopher Bertrand Russell (d. 1970): science tells us how things really are and as it progresses it gradually replaces commonsense knowing, which it shows to be illusory and false. But another major epistemological problem arising from the growth of modern science seems, as Russell well knew, to spoil this triumphalistic account of the onward march of science, as it reveals more and more truths about the world. Is not science intrinsically revisable? Is it only at best the best opinion of the day? How do we know, then, that it does reveal the world to us?

Even up until the twentieth-century positivist philosophers of science like Ernst Mach (d. 1916) held the view that science gives us certainty. But for a long time other philosophical schools of thought had pointed out that this was not so, and indeed, as the twentieth century went on, even the hard-nosed philosophers of science had to admit this was true. At present, the philosophy of science is divided between complete subjectivists, relativists, and instrumentalists on the one hand and realists on the other. But in the latter camp we do not find defenders of Mach's idea. Rather, we find various attempts to explain why we should hold that, why it is reasonable to think that, science does indeed progress and that its theories are probably true of reality.

That we do not have certainty in experimental science was a view held by some on the authority of Aristotle. Now, there is some ambiguity in Aristotle's thinking, it would appear, and this ambiguity or ambivalence with regard to experimental science is thought to have caused many of the tensions in the history of the development of science. On the one hand, in the *Posterior Analytics II*, Aristotle seems to say that true knowledge is certain knowledge of the causes of things and that this can only be had in definite metaphysical knowledge of the world. Some think that this Aristotelian position put the dampers on the growth of modern science, as scientific experiment does not give us certain knowledge but only probable knowledge at best. This was a point that some of Galileo's (d. 1642) critics made in the early seventeenth century when Galileo argued, like the ancient Greek Paul of Samosata, that the earth went around the sun, not the sun around the earth. Apart from other problems having to do with the case Galileo made, detractors could say, "Well, that is only a hypothesis, not a fact." Why can one say this? The point is a fairly simple one in logic. When you are trying to establish the cause of something you are trying to establish it as true that "if $A$ then $B$." But we do not directly see such connections in science between $A$, which is our hypothesis or explanation, and $B$, which is the data to be explained. We make inferences from $B$ to $A$ as being the best explanation of $B$. But we are not certain. Further, confirmation of any theory is only indirect. So if my hypothesis is that the fullness of the moon is the cause of Uncle Fred's taking three sugars in his tea, I can falsify the hypothesis, since one occasion on which Uncle Fred takes three sugars in his tea and there is not a full moon will be enough to show that there is not a hard-and-fast causal link between the two events. On the other hand, there is no knockdown way of confirming the causal link: okay, each time so far that Uncle Fred has taken the three sugars rather than the usual one in his tea has been an occasion on which there is a full moon. But that does not prove that there might be an occasion in the future when one sugar is taken and tea sipped in the light of a full moon. The causal link is not proven by a number of occasions on which both happen.

So the Aristotelians had their point. On the other hand, there are statements in Aristotle, and works of his on scientific matters, that imply that probable knowledge is still worth having, is still rational knowledge. So in *Ethics* he says that not every cognitive discipline should aspire to the same kind of certainty as mathematics, and in his work *On Meteors* he shows that he takes the way of probable explanation of some phenomena.

How should we handle questions concerning how things appear to common sense and how they are in themselves explained by science?

On the position taken in this book, reality, the real, is what we come to know through the use of our intelligence and reason. This is true with regard to both commonsense and scientific judgments concerning reality. Both scientists and ordinary folk can be attentive or inattentive to the data; they can try or fail to try to be as intelligent as possible in thinking up theories concerning the data; and they can be reasonable or rash in their judgments as to whether their ideas really correspond with the way reality is. Science grows out of common sense and uses the intelligence we can all employ, or fail to employ, in common sense to reach its conclusions. So both the scientist working in theories in quantum mechanics and the ordinary person trying to work out why her friend has been looking sad recently have to be attentive, intelligent, and reasonable if they want to come to a correct knowledge of the state of affairs.

It is quite false to think that science alone knows reality and common sense only knows appearance. It is true that science as a specialization aims to understand things in an explanatory way, things as related to one another, irrespective of a human observer and her interests. Commonsense knowing, on the other hand, is busy with the world of ordinary life. But when we make the commonsense judgment, "There is an oak tree by the house," we are not talking of an illusion or of a hallucination—not ordinarily anyway. Rather, the judgments may or may not give us a true statement about part of reality. Now, the scientist may go on from there to give us the latest theory about the differentiation in the evolutionary scheme in which oak trees have their place, or some such theory she takes to be probably true of reality. But this does not make our initial statement false or illusory. On the contrary, it presupposes the truth of the claim that there is an oak tree. Apparent conundrums about which of two statements is true in the case of "the earth revolves around the sun" or "the sun rises in the East, crosses the sky of the earth, and goes down in the West" can be settled if we realize that both are or can be true. But we need to recognize that, whereas the first is true as a statement about the solar system and the relative movements of its planets considered in itself, the second is true as an accurate statement of what things look like from the viewpoint of an observer on earth.

The world is known through science, common sense, scholarship, and in other ways. Each has a valid contribution to make. One thing we can think of here is that science is concerned with general statements. It is unlikely that in any scientific account one will have the judgment that a butterfly flew past the number 29 exit sign on the M1 at 9:57 on the morning of Wednesday, July 9, 2008. Now science is concerned with the life and habitats of butterflies, and theories are built up and tested with regard to particular instances. So the incident I mention *could* appear in some evidence-gathering log of a field scientist. But since I was there at the time, and no field scientist was in evidence, it is my commonsense report that provides knowledge of that moment in the history of the world, not any scientific account that might be invoked to explain why this particular species is attracted to motorway exit signs on warm summer mornings. But that still would not be the judgment, the knowledge of reality that *this* particular butterfly was at *this* particular location at *this* particular time.

Finally, in considering knowing and science we turn to the issue of the probable nature of scientific theory and the inherent revisability of science.

If I deny that I make judgments, it can be pointed out to me, I can notice, that in the very act of this denial I make a judgment. That is to say, the attempt to deny or argue against the truth that there are conscious cognitional acts in the process of coming to know only serves to show that there definitively are. For I find definitively that the conscious act of judgment is given in the data of my conscious activities when I attempt to deny that I do make judgments. Such definitive knowledge is not the case with scientific theories. I do not find that I am in contradiction with immediately given data of consciousness or any other data if I deny the latest scientific theory about why green leaves come out of the brown wood of this twig.

Scientific theory is, then, reasoning, making an inference to the best explanation of why the data are as they are. It is akin to the reasoning we see in the Sherlock Holmes stories and in this case we can say that only God knows "who done it," that is, what the explanation is of the *x* or *y* in a definitive or certain way. In the history of science, then, we see how a theory like oxygen gradually gained acceptance over older theories such as phlogiston, because the oxygen theory explained more and explained it more simply. This makes sense in terms of rational judgment. If I have enough evidence to make the probable judgment that one human being was responsible for this theft, I may or may not have sufficient evidence to judge that two or ten or twenty were jointly responsible. This is the criterion sometimes called Ockham's razor: one should not multiply causes without necessity.

If science is inherently revisable, this entails that further down the road there could be a better theory that replaces the theory we have now on something. But this still means that we can say of present scientific theory that it is probably true of reality. Some scientific accounts are more probable than others. So whatever the fate of some present theories, such as string theory in subatomic physics, may turn out to be, it is far less likely that radical revision will occur in our view that our solar system is part of a much larger universe than it will in string theory.

Since we are talking of probable judgments in science this may be a good place to make a few observations about probable judgments in general. Sometimes in the context of the "lazy relativism" of our culture (that is, the un-thought-out, dogmatic, and irrational relativism that some espouse) the impression is given that if we do not have certain or definitive knowledge of something, then we have only probable judgments in terms of our opinions which are subjective, wishy-washy "feelings that" and that all these feelings are equally valid. Now I do not wish to spend time debunking such notions as a whole since that has already been done in this text. But we can reflect a little on what is a probable judgment in terms of contrasting it with confused notions. A probable judgment is a rational claim about what is probably true of reality. Like the verdict in a courtroom, it is a reasoned assessment of evidence for a certain position. In real life we know the difference between opinions that have some reason to them and mere "feelings that," which we treat as completely off-the-wall or even morally dangerous. So when we have an argument about, say, the readiness of our football team to go into the next season, we and our friends who share the same enthusiasm argue on the basis of evidence over which we have some mastery. If someone in the room puts forward opinions in terms of their feelings that now we are doomed since more fair-haired players have been bought by the club than dark-haired players, we may be polite and respectful, but let us be honest in admitting that we do not hold that this is as "good" or equally valid an opinion as some more significant or well-founded views put forward in the debate. And if the individual in question carries on about his theory interminably, and our charity does not lapse, we are likely to move the conversation on to other topics or move deftly to another room.

If opinions, then, as probable judgments are, or can be, intelligent and reasonable, we can also explain why we think them probable and not certain or definitive. For to offer a probable judgment of varying degrees is to be aware that it is not certain, and therefore we are aware of truth as certain knowledge, as the standard relative to which a judgment is probable. What if someone were to object that the facts of cognitional structure themselves might only be probable, not certain? In response we can point out that we know these facts precisely as definitive, for we can understand that in showing that a claim like "I make no judgments" is false and incoherent we advert to an actual judgment occurring in this very case. There is no question that a judgment occurs in this case in my consciousness. The attempt to deny it shows that it occurs. It is precisely relative to such an instance that we can come to understand what a probable judgment is. For in a probable judgment we are aware that not all the evidence is in as it is in such cases of self-affirmation of the knower. How does that objector know that his judgment about cognitional structure is probable and not, perhaps, improbable or false? The fact is, offering a probable judgment is a matter of consciously giving reasons for why *x* might be the case, and it also involves awareness that these reasons are not complete or sufficient relative to cases in which the evidence is in in a complete or definitive manner.

## Insight in History

In this section we are going to consider briefly insight and human understanding and knowing in history and art. Again, in the brief comments offered, our interest will be in some features of these areas of human thought and life that throw light on common features in human knowing.

The first point to make about the inquiry of the historian is that it is a matter of attention to the data, intelligence in thinking up explanations for the data, and reasonableness in judging if those explanations are true or probably true, just as I have to go through these processes in ordinary life to increase the likelihood of knowing the truth, and just as the scientist has to go through such processes to know the truth concerning physical reality. The historian's judgments are probable with varying degrees of probability, just as the scientist's judgments are. For the historian's judgments are based on the available evidence for what was going forward, what were the significant developments in the past. We cannot see or smell or taste or touch the past, for the past does not now exist. The past did exist, but it no longer exists. Therefore, the probable nature of the judgments of the historian have this added aspect to them: they regard a past that we cannot directly inspect. This aspect of historical judgments caused difficulty for the logical positivists in the earlier part of the twentieth century, since their idea of knowing was empiricist: reality is the out there now real. In Wittgenstein's the *Tractatus* we see this bias as he says that the totality of true propositions about the world are the truths of physical science. Where does that leave history?

It was due to problems such as these (and due to its own internal consistency) that philosophers abandoned logical positivism. On the view we have argued in this book, reality is known through intelligent understanding and correct judgment on the basis of the data. In light of this we can see that history is as rational an inquiry as any other. For the historian makes inferences to what was going forward in the past on the basis of evidence presently available. Such evidence includes the recollections of living witnesses, the artifacts from archaeological investigation, ancient or more recent manuscripts, the traditions concerning the past handed down in copies of older written works, and in inscriptions on monuments and the like. It can also include evidence from dendrochronology or ice deposits concerning the climate in the past, since this will have had an important impact on human life and on human cultures.

In intelligently and reasonably sifting the data, the historian and community of historians will also be involved in a critical evaluation of sources. The experience that one soldier has of a battle is an important source for the historian. But the individual's experience is limited to his corner of the action. So the experiences of individuals involved in the battle need to be taken with all kinds of other sources of evidence if one is to understand the course and outcome of the battle and its significance for the war. Historians critically interrogate evidence from the past, just as detectives do in hunting for a criminal. The philosopher Karl Popper (d. 1994) thought that the data for historians is primed and "prejudiced" in a way that the physical data for the scientist is not. He thought this because the evidence of eyewitness accounts, letters, writings, inscriptions on monuments, and so forth is already constructed with human value judgments and perspectives on the data. This is no doubt true. But Popper overlooked the fact that historians try to be aware of this and use the data in a critical manner. So, for example, the letters of soldiers to loved ones at home during a war will contain the perspectives of the individual. But the historian may interrogate these to find evidence on social attitudes to the family at this period, or on the diet of the soldiers at the front: were they being well provisioned at this time? An answer to this could be important in understanding reasons why one side in a war was not doing so well. In other words, historians can interrogate the data to find out things that were not really in the forefront of the individual's mind at all when he wrote his letters home.

Both scientists and historians aim to come to know reality. Historians aim to know something of what was going forward during some period of the human past. Fundamentally, history is an attempt to answer the question, "Why are things as they are in the human world around us?" Both historians and scientists work in a community of fellow inquirers; they build on the work of previous generations, sometimes making small- or large-scale revisions of previous views. There are differences, however. For one thing, historians, like social scientists, study the collective life of human beings, whereas scientists, like physicists or biologists, do not. So for historians, human values and meanings are very important. To understand why $x$ or $y$ happened you may need to know what was the value, the end in view that a person or a community had in doing something. A further difference is that historians do not use a technical language as do scientists; one can enter the study of history at any point in the historical time scale, whereas in science one has to build up knowledge from the more simple to the more complex theories and practices.

## Insight and Art

To conclude this chapter we will consider a few points in order to illustrate human understanding and art.

If one thinks of human knowing or understanding as a matter of having a string of concepts that are like definitions in a dictionary, then one will tend to talk of art as if it were in opposition to knowing. Knowing is "logical," it is about concepts, whereas the experience of art, aesthetic experience, is just about "feelings," and it is "subjective." What we have studied in this book so far should help us to question such stereotyping of things. For one thing, as we have seen, the way "subjective" and "objective" are used can sometimes be misleading. It is not that science is "objective," whereas ordinary thinking is "subjective." Both the scientist and the person of common sense need to be, and ought to be, attentive, intelligent, reasonable, and responsible in trying to know the truth of the matter, whether this truth be the nature of a black hole or why my colleague looks particularly cheerful today.

Further, when we come to art as feeling and emotion, we need to be equally cautious. Yes, of course, feelings and emotions are central to this part of life, but equally central is human understanding. In the previous chapter we briefly looked at the distinction Lonergan makes on the second level in the process of coming to know, between conscious insight or the act of understanding on the one hand and the conscious activity of concept formulation or verbalization of insights on the other. Now, sometimes our insights may be so fleeting that we never formulate them into concepts, and at other times, as our examples in the previous chapter illustrated, we can find it difficult to formulate our insights into conceptual packages. We need to stress here that insights are not unconscious and concepts, conscious. Rather, if I am trying to get across to somebody something I understand, I sometimes experience frustration at not being able to put the thing into words in the best possible way. But my frustration is quite conscious, not unconscious. I am aware of what I want to say and of the shortcomings of the way I am saying it. If one has children between the ages of six and ten one will from time to time have the experience of trying to reexpress in other words, words they can grasp, one's insights into the meaning of a word or phrase they want to understand. These attempts can sometimes be more or less successful and can illustrate the conscious frustration I am alluding to.

Human understanding includes, then, verbal expression and concepts such as one finds in the dictionary, concepts defined by common use or by, for instance, legal, scientific, mathematical, or even philosophical explanation. It also includes, however, conscious acts of understanding, insights into the data that may or may not be formulated in these ways. This distinction between insight and concept, found in Lonergan's Thomist-inspired philosophy, is very important when coming to grasp the nature of aesthetic experience or art. This is because art is a matter not only of feeling but of understanding. I can walk down a street in a country that is very foreign to me, and I can see that certain things are quite evidently billboards that are advertising items. Now advertisements are aesthetic constructs: they appeal to us on the level of feelings. But they also "insinuate" or suggest to us insights. And this point can come home to us in the example I am using of an experience in a foreign land. For, although I recognize the thing as a billboard, I can say it means nothing to me, I do not understand it, I have no insight into it. And therefore it does not educe the kind of feelings in me that a person of that country might have in seeing it. Not only do I not understand the language but I may not understand the cultural significance of the facial expression of the person featured in the ad; and I may not understand that this was some politician who was a film star. So any jokes or double meanings used in the advertisement will be lost on me.

This simple illustration, then, brings to our attention the fact that aesthetic products and expressions, even those of far more value than a street advertisement, are a communication of both feeling and insight. The composer or sculptor will have insights and intelligent schemes in mind when he or she works on some artistic project, and, no doubt, these will be modified as the work progresses. But the composer or sculptor may find it quite difficult to express conceptually all the significant insights expressed in the artistic creation. In an interview about their work they may be more or less loquacious, or they may even be quite taciturn or say that they want the work to "speak for itself." The art critic or music scholar will be concerned with explicit, verbal, and conceptual accounts of what is expressed in the work of art, and will be concerned with making judgments about the worth of the artwork—the artist will also be concerned with evaluating the work, of course. We may find such art "appreciation" helpful or unhelpful; we may agree or disagree with its conclusions. But the point we are stressing here is that we can see the epistemological distinction between conscious insight and conscious conceptualization in the distinction between the direct creation of the artwork and our experience of it on the one hand

and, on the other, our, the artist's, or the scholar's or critic's conceptual evaluation of it.

In the creation of an artwork, a poem, a piece of music, a painting, or a film the artist wishes to pattern the data in accord with an insight he or she has and to communicate this to us. William Wordsworth wrote of his writing of poetry, of the process of aesthetic creation, as "emotion recollected in tranquillity." Now, he did not merely want to remember how he felt after a beautiful walk in the Lake District, but he wanted to express in words that would evoke certain feelings the insights he had enjoyed as he experienced nature. The philosopher of art, Susanne Langer (d. 1985), talks of art as being "the objectification of experiential patterns." In that way, she tries to indicate that our emotional experiences of something are what we attempt to express through the insight that gives an intelligible pattern to these colors or these sounds. So we recognize sounds in music that are now inspiring and glorious, now quiet and intimate, now sad and tragic. Music, in its patterns, expresses these aspects of our lives through the imitation of the ebb and flow of the emotions and feelings we experience in conjunction with events of life.

*Chapter 4*

# Positions on the Theory of Knowledge

## The Theory of Knowledge in the History of Philosophy

In previous chapters we have seen outlined and defended a basic position on the theory of knowledge and on our ability to come to objective knowledge. We have seen how this position can be defended, since its basic outlines cannot be denied or argued against without self-refutation: arguing against the basic position simply provides more evidence that it is correct. While this basic position can always be filled out further, the fundamental point is that it is not to be gainsaid: I cannot judge that I do not judge, and so on.

In previous chapters the concern has been to outline and defend the position taken without too much attention being given to other philosophical viewpoints, although naturally some of these, like empiricism, have been discussed. In order to deepen our understanding and appreciation of the nature and implications of the position taken so far, however, it will now be important to place it in the context of the wider history of philosophy and current philosophical debates. The treatment in this chapter will aim to do this, but it will be relatively brief. Our purpose here will be to concentrate on the theory of knowledge in the history of philosophy, and it will have a critical aspect to it. We want to give some very general guidance as to how, building on the positions argued for in this work, we could engage in debate with various philosophical options to see their strengths and weaknesses.

One very important thing to bear in mind is this: what has been argued so far about human knowing and objectivity has made a direct reference, a direct appeal, to your ability to confirm, to verify, the basic stance taken in your own conscious experience. The aim, then, has been the very personal one of self-discovery, of recognizing something important about yourself that makes explicit what you have been doing implicitly, but consciously, for years. That is the decisive issue: can this be verified in your consciousness? We have not, therefore, begun with a long discussion of the different positions of human knowing in philosophy in the past and present. We have not followed a method of outlining views and then begun a process of criticizing this point and that. For one thing, this can immediately create an impression in students of philosophy that there is just a succession of viewpoints that we can pick holes in, and that all this philosophy about human knowing may as well be talking about the dark side of the moon: it has nothing to do with me, with my life and existence. The immediate appeal to personal experience has had an existential, personalist thrust to it, then. And it has certainly not been an appeal to experience in a way that simply asks for your feelings or your vague opinion about $x$ or $y$. Rather, the appeal to experience, to your experience, has been in terms of asking you to verify cognitional fact, reality, in the data of your own consciousness. And it has drawn attention to the way identifying the stages in coming to know in your experience, data of consciousness, is a case of coming to know reality. The challenge of saying that to deny the basic account of knowing on three levels, or in three phases, or denying that we reach objectivity since this will lead to incoherence (for example, "it is truly the case that I cannot know what is truly the case") is a challenge to oneself.

Not only does the "let's see what they said and pick holes in it" approach to studying epistemology render the subject distant from the person studying it, but it can conceal a certain intellectual dishonesty, or inauthenticity. On what grounds do you or I do the "hole picking" in the positions of philosophers of the past or present? As the German philosopher Hegel said, "All negation is determinate." In other words, we criticize or pick holes from some position, from some standpoint. And if our criticism of other views is well-founded then that says something about the well-foundedness, the foundations, of our conscious experience of being able to criticize. We are at once back to cognitional theory and looking at our native, conscious ability to question, to ask for sufficient reason for $x$, to ask if $x$ is probable or certain, and so forth. We cannot pretend that we do not use these capacities to give rational criticism of other views. So we need to try to develop a view that is based precisely on that capacity for rational criticism: that is the position on cognitional theory and objective knowledge that has been our concern so far.

We will, then, clarify by comparison and contrast the position argued so far against certain key opposing views on knowledge in the history of thought. The focus will, however, in this brief history, be on areas of disagreement. This is in order to highlight the meaning and importance of the position we have argued. If that is the case, then we should also bear in mind the following points:

- There may be much else in the position of the philosopher or philosophers we are discussing that we would want to agree with regarding other areas of philosophy and even with regard to knowledge. It is unlikely that there is not some truth in any philosophical position.

- If we had more space, it would be well worth the effort to identify certain positive positions, even of the philosophers we disagree with more strongly. One could then invite or show the way to develop what is positive in these positions.

- We will not try to justify it here, but it is worth noting that the kind of position we are arguing for in this book sees a history of truth. In other words, it is not only the case that truths are to be found in philosophers that we may feel were mostly mistaken, but that the good points of any philosopher can be further developed insofar as they are true to begin with. This view contrasts both with the views of many philosophers in "modernity" and in "postmodernity." A number of key philosophers in the modern period, philosophers from the Enlightenment like Voltaire (d. 1778) or David Hume and those who react against them like postmoderns such as Michel Foucault (d. 1984) and Jacques Derrida (d. 2004), go for a view that really implies that nearly all of what was said in the philosophical past is rubbish. Now this itself is ironic, because the postmoderns are meant to be attacking the pride of people in the eighteenth century who thought themselves better than their forebears. And certain postmoderns want to say, "Let's return to the premoderns. Let us be more humble than the Enlightenment philosophers." But at the same time, some postmoderns (not all, by any means) like Foucault and Derrida really are saying that since we cannot have serious objective knowledge, a good deal of the philosophical past is written off, and now only they know what is best: only they are the enlightened ones. A position, on the contrary, that argues that there are both truths and errors throughout philosophy is, despite initial appearances to the contrary, less excessive in its claims than this latter position.

- Nevertheless, let us make no mistake, as the existentialists point out to us, once we are in this game there is no escape. You cannot avoid taking some position with regard to the views of someone. The absurd, lazy, and escapist "they are all as good as each other" attempted cop-out taken by some in contemporary culture is shown for what it is: incoherent. For this is precisely taking a position against any (and there would be many in the history of thought) view that opposes it. And even if you try to escape from the game, you cannot. That is, if you try to return, say, to early infancy when you never asked any of these questions, you will only be doing this *because* you want to escape, because you see that as a good *reason*, or a value.

## A Model or Map for Understanding Our Tour through the History of Epistemology in Philosophy

Below you will find a model or map that, it is hoped, will facilitate your understanding of some of the general or salient trends evident in the theory of knowledge in the history of philosophy. The trend or tradition argued for in this work so far has been that of Aristotelian-Thomism, particularly as this has been developed in light of modern thought by such philosophers as Lonergan.

| Platonism; seventeenth-century rationalism; some nineteenth-century idealists | Aristotelian and Thomist families of philosophy | Empiricism | Skepticism |
|---|---|---|---|
| • Knowledge as a priori (what is already there).<br><br>• Knowledge is innate in the sense that we have innate, inborn ideas. | • We do not have inborn, innate ideas but inborn, innate, dynamic principles, operative principles with which we come at the data to gain knowledge, | • Knowledge as a posteriori (what comes after).<br><br>• In this family of philosophies, ancient and modern, the attempt is to say that knowledge is | • Can be of various kinds but usually feeds off the struggle between Platonic type theories and empiricist.<br><br>• Hume, in the eighteenth |

| | | | |
|---|---|---|---|
| • Coming to know is in a way "remembering" these ideas (for Platonists, at least).<br><br>• In Kant (idealism), what is inborn are categories or patterns by which we structure what comes in through the senses—think of the patterns you can make in dough with different-shaped cutters giving you different-shaped biscuits. | for example, questioning; every child does this. Awareness of when the evidence is insufficient or when it is getting stronger in making a judgment of truth.<br><br>• For St. Thomas "nothing is in the intellect which is not first in the senses." But the intellect is already a dynamic power or set of powers. | just what comes into our minds through the five senses.<br><br>• There is a bit of organization allowed, of course, but this is kept to a minimum.<br><br>• Nothing is innate or already there in the mind. | century, pushed empiricism as far as he could and then ended in skepticism. Why? Because if you really only just have the data from the senses, all you know of the world is bits of color, bits of sound, and so on. |

The model provides a sketch of this history in very broad brush strokes, and one needs to be aware of its limitations. For one thing, individual philosophers can combine and mix elements from the various trends listed. Furthermore, to talk of an "Aristotelian-Thomist" tradition can, to some extent, be misleading. St. Thomas changed and added to Aristotle's position, and nineteenth- to twenty-first-century philosophers inspired by Aquinas's thought engage in extremely lively debates and disagreements on various points. Having said all this, however, I think it is true to say that the agreements are more significant than the disagreements, especially when one looks at the "tradition" from the outside, from the perspective of other philosophical options. With such reservations in mind it is, however, helpful to remember the model as we proceed on our whistle-stop tour of the history of epistemology that will follow.

You will notice in the column marked "Aristotelian-Thomism" that what is stressed is the fact that there are not inborn ideas, but rather innate, operative principles: dynamic conscious orientations that characterize the mind, the intellect. These are precisely what we have been discussing when we examined cognitional structure. That is, the conscious structure of our minds as moving toward truth about reality through our asking What? questions, and Is it true? questions. Below, we shall examine in a little more detail the way Aquinas identifies such operative, conscious principles of the mind, using Latin metaphysical terminology. We shall also see how, in philosophers such as Hume, the attempt to employ a highly simplified empiricist model of the mind results in skepticism, which is ultimately self-destructive: if that is really the way the mind is, Hume cannot even arrive at the few results on which he bases his own skeptical account.

## A Whistle-Stop Tour of the History of Epistemology

### *From Socrates to Ockham*

The cradle of Western philosophy, as of much of Western culture, is fourth- to fifth-century Greece. The key figures in this story are Socrates, Plato, and Aristotle. Before these thinkers, about whom we know a fair deal, there were other thinkers, known as the pre-Socratics, who speculated on the nature of the world; what little we know of their thought indicates that it was a mixture of what we might now separate as science and philosophy. There is a great deal of literature about the beginnings of philosophy in the West. One thing seems evident: there were political and social tensions in the world of ancient Greece, and one can understand Socrates' attempts to get at a clearer understanding of important ideas of an ethical nature that circulated in everyday discussions in order to gain clarity in a situation in which old ideas and ways of acting were being challenged. We know about Socrates and the discussions or dialogues he had with various people through the lens of his pupil Plato; it is Plato who gives us accounts of these discussions. In these debates, Socrates tries to get a clearer understanding of such concepts as "friendship," "courage," "good actions," "knowledge of virtue," and the like. His interlocutors often become frustrated by his repeated questions, and in many of the dialogues Socrates fails to get at any definite answers. But one thing he is definite about is that one should pursue truth. In this his opponents are the *Sophists*. Many of them present arguments to the effect that truth is unattainable as people of different cultures (there were many such in the known world) see things differently, and so do individuals. There is no objective truth, but what we need to do is to teach people how to debate and argue, so that they can become useful civil servants. Socrates will have none of this: the claim that there is no objective truth *is itself a claim to know an objective truth—all relativism is self-destructive.*

In the works of Plato and Aristotle we find more full-blown and extensive philosophical discussion. In Plato we see a theory of knowledge develop that emphasizes the way our minds grasp the "form" or idea of something that is then applied to many material instances of that same thing in the world. So we learn the "form" or idea of "horse" or "table" or "man," and then we apply them to the many individuals we come across who fit the bill. Plato thus develops an *epistemology* (from the Greek word *episteme*, "to know"), or theory of knowledge. This theory of knowledge becomes linked to a general theory of reality, or a *metaphysics*. These two areas are two of the crucial areas discussed in philosophy. Plato links them (and as we shall see, they are always interlinked) by arguing that there are aspects of our ability to know that suggest that we do not get all that we know from the outside world; rather we have some *innate* capacities that are inborn. This is another area of dispute that keeps recurring throughout the history of philosophy. Some philosophical views stress the importance for our knowledge of what comes in through our five senses: seeing, hearing, touching, tasting, and smelling. These views downgrade or even completely deny that there is something already in us that we bring to knowledge. *Empiricism* is the name given to such kinds of philosophy. A view like Plato's, however, seems to suggest that the outside world contributes far less to our knowledge. Plato even goes so far as to argue that we must have lived before, and that knowing as it occurs in this life is a kind of remembering what we have seen before birth, rather like one remembers the face of someone one has met in meeting them again. Plato thinks that we have seen the "forms" or "ideas" before; he holds to a kind of reincarnation doctrine. So we see the connection between epistemology (theory of knowledge) and metaphysics (theory of reality) in Plato. For he argues that reality is characterized by souls coming from some kind of heaven and being born and reborn into bodies in the earthly world.

Plato's view may seem rather far-fetched, and part of the problem is that one cannot do justice to it in a short summary. But there is *something* that is important in it that is taken up by Aristotle, Plato's pupil. Aristotle rejected Plato's theory of knowledge as remembering a previous life. He put much greater stress on the experience of this life and the material in coming to know. After all, he was trained as a man of science, a doctor, who was fascinated by the real world. He wrote on the movements of the planets (actually producing an ingenious argument for the world's being round), and he also studied animal behavior (fascinated by the movements of crabs). Aristotle has something in common with the empiricists then. But he does not go all the way with them. We do bring certain capacities with us to knowledge.

After all, Plato was surely wrong when he thought that somehow before birth we had seen the "great exemplar" of ideas like "elephant," "quasar," "ship," or "toothache" in heaven. But he was on to something when he asked: how do we know we have gotten to the truth when we get it? There is something innate in us. Aristotle noticed the way in which we have a terrific capacity to question, to wonder, which begins when we are small children; and he observed that such wonder is the beginning of all philosophy. Aristotle also retained Plato's notion of form as applying to the real world. Clearly, he argued, the real world does have this interesting characteristic: by understanding one form we can understand what may apply to many instances. One understands the form "atom" in science, and that applies to myriad instances of the same thing; if it did not, scientists would have to inspect every so-called atom in the world to see if they were significantly the same. One design of a chair or a woman's handbag can be realized in thousands of instances off the production line. So things are composed of "matter" and "form"; by matter we mean just this particular material instance. Aristotle also reflected on another aspect of reality: causes. He identified four different types of these. He also argued for some kind of God—not the God who creates "out of nothing," but a God who is more the governor or ruler of what goes on. From a reflection on man as a "rational animal," Aristotle also offered profound reflections on what constituted a good political society for human beings. Plato had already offered his rather different thoughts on this (he tends more to a totalitarian model, Aristotle to some kind of democracy) in his great work *The Republic*.

A fundamental difference between Plato's and Aristotle's theories of knowing can be brought out if we consider the story told in one of the Platonic dialogues, the *Meno*. In the *Meno* the group of Greek thinkers are considering the nature of learning, and they bring in an untutored slave boy in order to see how well he can solve a little puzzle in geometry. The boy tries to solve the puzzle by drawing different solutions or parts of solutions in the sand. Finally, he hits on the solution. The group is impressed that a lad unlearned in Euclid's geometry can, with a bit of prompting, solve a geometrical puzzle. The conclusion drawn in the dialogue is that since he did not learn this from teachers he must have had it from somewhere: he must have already had the idea in his mind from his previous life. But Aristotle might draw a very different lesson from the little story. The Aristotelian might concentrate on the fact of the boy's drawing different solutions or parts of projected solutions in the sand. This fiddling around with the images and diagrams is what facilitates insight into the data. This very physical operation is essential for human knowing. And it shows that this understanding is a new event, not just a remembering of something that was known before. The physical, material factors in human knowing will also be stressed by Aquinas, who will hold that in this life, for human beings, understanding is always through insight into the mental imagery. This very "physical side" to the Aristotelian-Thomist tradition makes it open to the kind of contributions that may be made to the study of human knowing and willing by twentieth-century philosophers such as the French philosopher Maurice Merleau-Ponty (d. 1961), who stressed the physicality and bodiliness of human perception.

In a whistle-stop tour such as this we must take great leaps and bounds across history. We pass over the developments of various schools of late Greek and Roman philosophy, when various forms of neoplatonism developed, and schools such as the Stoics and Cynics who reflected on human ethical life, to the dawn of Christianity. The greatest figure of the first thousand years of the church in the area of philosophy, a thinker who is important in the history of Western philosophy, is, of course, St. Augustine. A number of philosophical influences enter into his work, which is largely neoplatonic in form. But there is a highly original synthesis in Augustine's thinking. He is often called the first "existentialist," given that much of his philosophizing occurs in the context of a story of personal struggle and a quest for God, "the Beloved." He also seems to be the first person to have come up with the proof that people often think originated with René Descartes (d. 1650) in the sixteenth century: "I think, therefore I am." In other words, I cannot doubt my own existence, for when I doubt I have evidence of my existence. Augustine, however, uses the argument in a different way from Descartes. Augustine also reflected on space, time, and God. Interestingly enough, his views here were close to those of Einstein (d. 1955) and twentieth-century relativity. Augustine wrote that God does not create *in* time but *with* time—that is, unlike the picture in Newtonian physics, which Einstein replaced, time is not like a river flowing with God from all eternity, into which God pops the world and planets; rather, time is a creature that is created *with* the world.

The Catholic dialogue with philosophy continued on into the Middle Ages, which began with Augustine's form of neoplatonism being very influential in Christian circles, but with the presence of a number of other philosophical approaches also evident among theologians. The rediscovery of much of Aristotle's work, which came back into European academic circles accompanied by the commentaries of Arab, Muslim, and Jewish philosophers, proved profoundly important for the thought of *St. Albert the Great* (d. 1280) and his even greater pupil, St. Thomas Aquinas. St. Thomas tried to find a new way of integrating the Augustinian tradition with that of Aristotle and had to defend his position from certain Augustinians on the one hand and those who interpreted Aristotle according to the Muslim Averroes on the other. But St. Thomas's brilliant creative synthesis witnesses to a further point we have not yet brought out: Christian thought was not only a dialogue with a philosophy that stood outside it, but it itself made novel and creative contributions to human philosophy. So St. Thomas Aquinas, from a faith tradition that taught the absolute transcendence of a Creator God, went beyond the Aristotelian notion of a God who was a mere controller of events to argue philosophically for a God whose essence is pure existence, whose very nature is an infinitely dynamic act. In other areas also, the Christian tradition of reflection on faith, in such areas as that of reconciling divine care and Providence with human freedom, led St. Thomas to penetrate far more deeply than his predecessors into the analysis of human free acts. St. Thomas, like Aristotle, also wrote on political philosophy. Much of Aquinas's brilliance in philosophy occurs where he is using philosophical analysis in the context of reflecting on dogmas of faith. So some of his most original thought on the human mind and its capacities is found in passages on the Trinity. St. Thomas, developing insights from Aristotle and others, steered a middle course between Platonic theory of knowledge on the one hand and naive empiricism in epistemology on the other: he was a bold realist about our ability to know reality—God's creation.

Both Aristotle and Aquinas were clear on the capacity of the conscious mind to come to know itself. Like St. Augustine before him and Descartes after him, St. Thomas knew that the skeptic about knowledge becomes involved in self-contradiction: the man who claims it is true that there is no truth or that he cannot know the truth is involved in such a self-destructive argument, for he himself is making a judgment or truth claim.

At this point we can usefully look forward in history to Descartes' argument that I can have certain knowledge of myself and to the criticisms of this idea found in nineteenth-century philosophers like Friedrich Nietzsche (d. 1900) and twentieth-century philosophers like Ludwig Wittgenstein, and compare and contrast these views with those of St. Thomas on certain knowledge of myself (views that enter into our position on cognitional structure and knowing). Descartes seemed to say that I can have immediate, certain knowledge of myself in the affirmation "I think, therefore I am," but later critics argue that, for instance, this knowledge is not immediate because it relies on words and language concepts that come from the outside, from my culture and society.

Thus, Nietzsche makes some telling points against versions of this argument, the most important being that this is not "immediate knowledge" at all. For to know something like "I think, therefore I am" one must already understand something about "thinking"—that it is not "willing," for example. One must have come to understand the concepts in use. If this is so, the "I think" is not immediate knowledge but shows a dependency on something else, on the prior conceptual understanding of words and concepts used.

Whether or not Nietzsche's presentation of Descartes' position does it justice is something I would leave to the Cartesian scholars. I would not myself wish to mount a defense of Descartes' general philosophical position, of which the *Cogito* argument forms a part, since I do not accept many of its fundamental tenets. For one thing, I agree with John Henry Newman that the method of doubt seems to exclude far too much if taken as a way to discover truth. And, indeed, the method itself leads one to doubt the method as a viable starting point (since it says "doubt everything that can be doubted!"). While I am not impressed by many aspects of Descartes' philosophy, however, I do remain convinced of the validity of some other versions of the argument that one can have certain knowledge of oneself and of one's intellectual operations and acts. Such arguments are also found in, for example, St. Augustine's *Contra Academicos* and in St. Thomas's *De Veritate*. Philosophers such as Peter Hoenen and the analytical philosopher Jaakko Hintikka have, in helpful ways, drawn attention to points of comparison and contrast between St. Thomas's argument for self-knowledge and that of Descartes. Indeed, Hintikka believes Aquinas's position is the stronger one primarily because it occurs in the context of St. Thomas's general philosophical position on knowledge of the soul, which denies that we have any direct intuition into the essence of our souls. Rather, knowledge of the soul, for St. Thomas, proceeds in the following way: we move from knowledge of the objects that are the aim of our intellectual acts to attention to those acts themselves and from them conclude to the faculties of the soul (cf. *In III de Anima*, lect. 9, 724; *In III Sent.*, 23, 1). The kind of "immediate certainty" regarding the self or "I think" that Nietzsche denies is also denied by St. Thomas. It is perhaps interesting to note that the postmodern French philosopher Derrida in his study of Edmund Husserl's philosophy, *Speech and Phenomena*, also takes issue with Husserl's claim to reach a direct, unmediated intuition into the self in this way. For Derrida, as for Nietzsche, there is an inescapable element of dependency from which any putative direct intuition cannot escape, since the knowledge of the self depends on the concepts employed such as "I" and "thinking," and these concepts arise from a prior process of understanding.

St. Thomas at once acknowledges this dependency of the concepts used in affirmations concerning the self and its acts, and at the same time insists that certain knowledge is possible in this area. In *De Veritate* he affirms: "In this respect the science of the soul is most certain inasmuch as each one experiences in himself that he has a soul and that the acts of the soul are present in him" (*"Secundum hoc scientia de anima est certissima, quod unusquisque in seipso experitur se animam habere, et actus animae sibi inesse"* [*De Veritate*, q.10, a.8; see also *In De Anima*, lect. 1, n. 6]). Hoenen is in agreement with Hintikka that St. Thomas's argument in *De Veritate* occurs in the wider context of his general philosophical position on the way we come to have knowledge of the soul. In that process we can, as Aristotle affirms, sense our sensing, understand our understanding, and come to know other acts of our minds (*Ethics* IX, 9; 1170a 31). It is no surprise, then, that we approach the argument as to the impossibility of denying our own existence through a process in which we come to understand the concepts employed, and Nietzsche's objection serves to draw our attention to this fact. A further refinement observed in St Thomas's argument in *De Veritate*, by Hintikka, which he believes is lacking in Descartes, draws our attention to the fact that this is not certainty based on the immediate intuition of some self-evident truth and indicates the correct manner of understanding the argument. In *De Veritate* St. Thomas writes that one can in fact think the proposition "I exist" as untrue (*DV*, q. 10, a. 12, ad. 7). It is a contingent proposition, and one can entertain the thought, as a possibility, of one's nonexistence. But it is when, and precisely when, one puts forward this thought with assent, *cum assensu*, that one lands in contradiction. Why? Because the act of making the judgment, the affirmation "I do not exist," is precisely the kind of conscious act that shows that I do exist. For this act is also connected with other intellectual acts of the soul, such as questioning and grasping concepts, and therefore the occurrence of such acts, even in the moment of self-denial, is evidence that the thinking self exists.

St. Thomas employs Latin metaphysical language to speak of the *intellectus agens* (the agent intellect) and the *intellectus possibilis* (the possible intellect), and he identifies the two fundamental types of questions we have referred to already (the *Quid sit*? [What is it?] question and the *An sit?* [Is it so?] question), and he speaks of the process of coming to make judgments as that of "composition and division," *compositio vel divisio*. Such Latin metaphysical jargon can be complex and confusing, especially when scholars are attempting to see if and when there is development in Aquinas's own thinking. But it may well be that the variety of such terminology is indicative of an extremely subtle and even accurate identification of our intellectual processes. In the nineteenth and twentieth centuries there occurred a revival of interest in the thought of Aquinas and other medievals. This was not at first "church driven" at all. In fact, Catholic theologians at the beginning of the nineteenth century used the works of all kinds of philosophers, while in some pockets attachment to medieval thinkers like Aquinas had not died out. Rather, as a reaction to eighteenth-century Enlightenment thought and as increased historical awareness of medieval philosophy grew, there was a sense among some philosophers inside and outside the Catholic Church that there were great philosophical resources to be used in a creative fashion to dialogue with contemporary philosophical trends.

Eventually Pope Leo XIII issued the encyclical *Aeterni Patris* in 1879, which officially encouraged this movement, while at the same time he also encouraged other philosophical approaches, as was evident from his making Newman a cardinal in that year. Newman followed a different path from that of scholastic philosophy. It is perhaps interesting to note that Lonergan, whose approach we follow, brings together aspects of Newman's thought with those of Aquinas.

After this philosophical discussion ranging across several centuries, and a digression into Catholic studies in the nineteenth and twentieth centuries, we should return to our chronological path. The thirteenth and fourteenth centuries witnessed movements in philosophy in Catholic Europe that were very different and indeed at variance with the position taken by Aquinas. So we see the rise of what is called "nominalism" in philosophy and the work of Blessed Duns Scotus (d. 1308) and William of Ockham (d. 1349). There is a great stress by these thinkers on logic, but it may be asked whether they lose sight of some of the more subtle positions evident in Aquinas on theory of knowledge and metaphysics. As we move from the late Middle Ages into the Renaissance, Catholic philosophy was further influenced by the "rediscovery" of Plato's works and a renewed interest in other ancient philosophical traditions such as Stoicism.

### From Descartes to MacIntyre

The new challenges emerging from the Reformation and the rise of modern science in the fifteenth to seventeenth centuries led to the philosophical systems of philosophers such as René Descartes. Descartes attempted to doubt all that was possible to doubt in order to find a firm foundation on which to base the new sciences. The sciences of physics, astronomy, and medicine were growing apace in this period, as were developments in mathematics, to which Descartes himself made valuable contributions. This was the time in which the work of Copernicus on the planets was being built on by Galileo Galilei, Johannes Kepler (d. 1630), and Tycho Brahe (d. 1601). Astronomers were benefiting from technological advances like the telescope and the microscope. In medicine, the Englishman William Harvey (d. 1657) made a great breakthrough with the discovery of the circulation of blood in the 1620s. It seemed that the old commonsense world was being dissolved by the new sciences. "How can one find certainty here?" it was asked: a certainty that will help us know that even our new scientific experiments are themselves not leading us off track. These were the questions that led Descartes into his attempt to doubt all that could be doubted in order to find a firm foundation on which to rebuild knowledge and science. But Descartes' attempt ran into problems. We saw how Augustine argued that one cannot doubt one's existence: fine. But having gotten this far, Descartes' philosophy made a rather weak jump from there to knowledge of the outside world on the basis of an argument for God's existence. He also presupposed a number of questionable things about how the world must be.

A further contrast between Descartes' *Cogito ergo sum* ("I think, therefore I am") argument and the cognitional structure we have examined in this book that might be useful to highlight has to do with the level of judgment. Some points about differences were made above in our discussion of St. Thomas's views on certain knowledge of the self. A further issue, however, is this: when pressed by his contemporaries to say how one would decide about other ideas besides the idea of myself in the "I think," Descartes could only reply that we need to test other ideas to see if they have the same clarity and distinctness as the "I think, therefore I am" idea of myself. This was unconvincing. The notion was that since I cannot doubt my own existence, the idea of my own existence is extremely clear and distinct, and other ideas could be tested for their truth insofar as they had similar or approximating degrees of clarity and distinctness about them. But the point is that I cannot doubt my own existence insofar as I cannot consistently make the judgment that I am not a knower: that I do not engage in the conscious activities on the three levels of coming to know. Why? Because in arguing against the claim that I am a knower in this sense, I find that the evidence is there that I do engage in these conscious activities. In other words what is clear and distinct is not simply an idea of myself, but rather that the evidence is in, the evidence of my conscious debating and questioning activities, for making the judgment that "I am a knower." Judgment is a matter of taking an idea and finding evidence for or against it. In the cases being discussed this is definitive: I cannot question it without showing the evidence is in. But in other cases I may have enough evidence for a probable judgment that something is so, or not so, about reality. Without this notion of judgment, judgment as grasping evidence for a definitive or probable judgment, Descartes is at a loss to say both how the "I think, therefore I am" argument is definitive and how other ideas may be said to be definite or probable. And of course, the "probable" is very important in modern science. It is no wonder, then, that part of Descartes' problem is that he cannot really say that science is rational or reasonable without at once demanding that it is completely certain, and he thinks he has to create an a priori science of the world, which is like mathematics, in order to provide the foundations for a true science.

A number of other thinkers followed his lead or took a similar track. This group is known as the seventeenth-century *rationalists*. Descartes is one of their number, which also includes the Jewish philosopher Baruch Spinoza (d. 1677), Gottfried Wilhelm Leibniz (d. 1716), Nicolas Malebranche (d. 1715), and Pierre Gassendi (d. 1655). Rather like Plato, these thinkers stressed the need to work out a general theory of reality based on what could be known through pure reflection, or discovery of innate ideas. These ideas would tell us in general fashion about the nature of reality; then the experimental methods of the new sciences could fill in the details. In reaction to this group we have a new wave of empiricists, often known as the *British empiricists*, of the seventeenth and eighteenth centuries. Beginning with Thomas Hobbes (d. 1679) and developing through John Locke (d. 1704), Bishop George Berkeley (d. 1753), and David Hume, these thinkers combined great admiration for the new sciences (especially as Isaac Newton's work began to win ground after the 1680s) with a resistance to the rationalists' attempt to sketch out some general theory of reality in advance of the sciences discovering things about the world.

So, in his *Essay Concerning Human Understanding*, Locke says that it is all very well to speculate across space, time, and infinity about the nature of the world, God, and so forth, but do we know if our minds are up to this task? He sets himself to study this question and emphasizes the way it is the material coming in through our senses that is crucial for knowledge. We then knit this together in various ways in order to come to know the world. A strong emphasis on empiricism, however, with its insistence on knowledge "coming in through the senses," soon leads, strange as it may seem, to skepticism about the real world. We see this in Berkeley and even more in Hume. For Hume, we pare things down until we just have colors, sights, sounds, and tastes in our knowledge. The knitting together of these things is just a *subjective* and *arbitrary* exercise, which we perform simply out of habit or custom. So, for instance, we do not know if there is a real cause-and-effect relationship between things in the world: we see this billiard ball touch that one, and we say the second one's moving is *caused* by the first one's hitting it; but we do not see any cause. Maybe tomorrow the second billiard ball will disappear back inside the first one—we do not know.

It is worth devoting a little more space to Hume, as he is key for what happens in the subsequent history of philosophy in both the Anglo-American sphere and the German and continental sphere. It is his skepticism with regard to Descartes and the rationalists that affects German philosophy in Kant and is continued in the English-speaking world to some extent by John Stuart Mill (d. 1873) and others.

Despite the impression Hume's writings might convey, his skepticism about the capacity of the human mind is anything but original. As we have seen, skepticism and relativism mark the very beginnings of philosophy, and there have been periods in which skeptical positions were dominant. Some forms of skepticism were combined with religious faith to form a kind of fideism. So in the tenth century certain Muslim philosophers expressed the same kind of doubts Hume would express about our capacity to know that there is real cause and effect in the world since, in their view, God could capriciously use causes between things in the world for a day or a period and then dispense with them, giving us the illusion that it was the wind that caused the door to open when really God did it directly. Similar forms of skepticism were expressed by Christian thinkers in the Middle Ages like Nicholas of Autrecourt (d. ca. 1369). As we have seen in the previous chapter, for those who stressed the Aristotelian idea that science had to be certain, this would be a problem: how could we be certain that *A* caused *B*? Yes, *B* followed *A* and kept following it. But how did we know there was any kind of real causal power between *A* and *B*? Perhaps God just kept the arrangement going and there was no causal influx. After all, we do not see such influxes directly. Other medieval philosophers, like Jean Buriden, responded that we should seek probable reasons here, not certainty. Hume's arguments to the effect that we do not see causes, therefore, were not as original as he was wont to suggest. In the chapter on metaphysics to follow we will take a critical look at what Hume has to say and on the way his epistemological views pan out in other areas of philosophy.

The empiricist attitude began to win support in Europe and replace rationalism. This took place in the movement that we call the *Enlightenment* of the eighteenth century. The Enlightenment was really a cultural movement in Europe at that time that wanted to spread the ideals it saw in the development of science to the rest of society. So old European institutions, customs, and the like had to be swept away in the name of new "rational scientific" approaches. We think particularly of French thinkers as being prominent in this movement: Voltaire, Étienne Bonnot de Condillac (d. 1780), Denis Diderot (d. 1784), Baron d'Holbach (d. 1789), and Jean-Jacques Rousseau (d. 1778). One of the ideas typical of the time was to produce an encyclopedia in which the leading lights of the day would spread the most up-to-date scientific information on economy, law, politics, and religion so as to bring about social reform. In this period, although many Enlightenment thinkers were believers, we see the spread of atheism, agnosticism, and materialism (man is just flesh and blood, not to survive death) among intellectuals. Religion was attacked by an increasing number as "superstition."

The irony is that Hume wanted to do for the study of human nature what Newton (d. 1727), a hero of his, had done for physical nature: reveal the laws that made them tick. But if Hume is right, Newton's science, or any science, is up the creek without a paddle: for if Hume is right, science cannot reveal causes of things in the real world. Immanuel Kant reacted against this antiscientific move in Hume. In his famous work, *The Critique of Pure Reason*, Kant tried to bring back the rational, well-founded status of Newton's science by arguing that our minds have a certain structure to them, and through this structure we organize the world. Part of that structure of the mind means that Newton's science, with its causes of things, and Euclid's geometry are built into the very way we have to divide up and understand the world. While Kant is a profound thinker and his other contributions in moral philosophy teach us a great deal, there are still deep problems with his enterprise, problems that we have looked at in earlier chapters: for ultimately Kant is holding the incoherent position that "it is really so, that I cannot know what is really so." What Kant kept from Hume was the idea that we do not really know reality, but we impose an order on it. This move was taken up by other thinkers in the period of German *idealism*. The most famous idealist after Kant is the German thinker Georg Wilhelm Friedrich Hegel. Hegel combines Kant's subjective views on knowledge with a massive account of human culture and history, a history that studies the way in which human beings increasingly discover their true identity through culture and philosophy. Other philosophers of this period include Johann Gottlieb Fichte (d. 1814), Friedrich Wilhelm Joseph von Schelling (d. 1854), and Arthur Schopenhauer (d. 1860). Idealism also spread and became influential in Britain, America, and other parts of Europe. Such idealism is simply the logical working out of the Hume-Kant starting point: I do not see that my seeing actually gets me to what I think I see, so I do not know reality. But knowing is not seeing. It is a compound of seeing and other sensitive activities, of understanding and of judging. While we can say that empiricists tend to stress the first—sensation, data, level of coming to know—and idealists want to correct this by pointing to the importance of what we bring to knowledge via understanding (in a way similar to Platonists and rationalists, but with differences: for example, the former two groups will say we do get to reality via our ideas; the idealists may say all we have is the ideas), we can say that both groups fail to appreciate the importance of judgment in coming to know. And it is precisely in their judgments that the two groups are seen to be incoherent. For they claim to know what is so, or they claim to know that their probable judgments are based on good reasons for saying what is probably the case. To know it is really the case, as an idealist does, that I know "appearance" and not reality is to claim to know what is really so—therefore it is not to be tricked by appearance.

To get to the heart of the issue we have to appreciate just why it is that Kant, or anyone trying to follow him, lands in the contradiction he does (and this point is not always properly appreciated). When I grasp that claiming "I cannot know what is really so" is incoherent and therefore not so, not true, what do I grasp? I grasp that a judgment, a conscious truth claim, has occurred (the claim to know that I do not know), so not only do I know the claim is false, but I only do so because I know some reality, that is, the reality of the conscious judgment that I have made in asserting "I cannot know what is so." I am back to the facts of cognitional structure, back to the facts of my conscious intelligent and reasonable operations that are the realities involved in this argument as in any other. Great and important as many other contributions are in modern and postmodern philosophy, insofar as this confused and crippling subjectivism is not overcome or gone beyond, philosophy has not really progressed in any deep sense beyond the confusions of Hume and Kant.

One positive feature of this period is a reaction against the biases of the eighteenth-century Enlightenment. Idealist philosophies develop at the time of European romanticism in art and literature, and there is a reevaluation of history, tradition, art, and religion. The empiricist and materialist tradition of the eighteenth century, however, is still strong: in France, in the work of Auguste Comte (d. 1857); in Britain, in the work of the utilitarians Jeremy Bentham (d. 1832) and John Stuart Mill; in Germany, above all in the work of Karl Marx (d. 1883). Marx combines Hegel's attempt to give an account of history and its development on a grand scale with eighteenth-century views on religion and the nature of the person as merely a material being.

Toward the end of the nineteenth century and at the beginning of the twentieth century there was a reaction against idealism. Thinkers more sympathetic to the tradition of British empiricism and Mill placed stress on the importance of science and scientific objectivity and reacted against idealism in much the same way as the seventeenth- and eighteenth-century empiricists reacted against rationalism. The view was now: "Let's forget about this armchair attempt to work out the structure of the world. Let's follow what the scientists are actually doing and learn lessons about objective knowledge from them." In Britain, philosophers like Bertrand Russell and G. E. Moore (d. 1958) led the attack against idealism. Against its "subjective stance" they urged commonsense realism, scientific objectivity, and, in the case of Russell, the importance of new work done in logic and mathematics. In the nineteenth century, much work had been done in formulating logic that could be expressed in mathematical symbols. The ideal was that we could reduce and express all we say in a long-winded way in ordinary talk to sets of symbols; that would also help us to see when we are talking sense and when nonsense.

Philosophers like Russell and the German Gottlob Frege (d. 1925) were important in this movement. An interest in language and its function and structure is very evident here. It was as a result of work on formulating symbolic expressions of what we say in language that ideas about the computer developed in the 1930s. And toward the end of the Second World War a computer was built. What we call the *Anglo-American tradition* of philosophy, which is still with us today, is marked by concerns with language, logic, and the methods of science. The Austrian Ludwig Wittgenstein (d. 1951) who came to England and studied with Russell and Moore was, in the first part of his career, dedicated to this logical dissection and mapping out of language. This he attempted in his *Tractatus* of 1922. But he became increasingly disenchanted with this ideal. Ordinary language, with its gestures and nuances of expression, is so very fluid, and logic cannot capture poetry and pin it down without destroying it. In his later work, *Philosophical Investigations*, he rejected the earlier "logical map" idea and looked at the various "language games" we are involved in. Wittgenstein was not alone here. Other British and English-speaking philosophers like Gilbert Ryle (d. 1976), John Wisdom (d. 1993), and John L. Austin (d. 1960) saw the importance of analyzing ordinary language in a way that could throw fresh light on old philosophical problems. This *linguistic analysis* was all the rage in English-speaking universities increasingly from the 1950s through the 1960s and 1970s, but it seems to have become somewhat overused. By the 1980s it was giving way to other philosophical approaches and interests in philosophy. Philosophy of science is still very important in Anglo-Saxon thought. The contributions of Karl Popper, Thomas Kuhn (d. 1996), Paul Feyerabend (d. 1994), and others have been notable here.

On the continent, however, things took a somewhat different direction. Franz Brentano (d. 1917), inspired by the medieval philosophers' subtle analyses of mental life and mental intentions, explored the inner world of the mind. Brentano taught both Sigmund Freud (d. 1939) and Edmund Husserl (d. 1938), the founder of the *phenomenological* movement in philosophy. Husserl went in for subtle, fine-grained analyses of our mental life or *intentional* acts, even investigating the various tones and nuances of what we actually hear when we hear the sound of, say, a crunching of the gravel outside on the path. Others in this movement, like Max Scheler (d. 1928), analyzed human emotions and feeling states. This movement developed into the offshoots of *existentialism* and *personalism*. In a sense, existentialism was already seen in St. Augustine and certainly in the nineteenth-century Christian thinkers Newman and the Danish Søren Kierkegaard (d. 1855). As a style of philosophizing, it is closer to the novel or the autobiography, placing concrete philosophical thoughts in the context of an actual life struggle. In existential thinkers like Martin Heidegger and Karl Jaspers (d. 1969) in Germany or Jean-Paul Sartre and Albert Camus (d. 1960) in France one sees descriptive accounts of human moods, experiences of being together (intersubjectivity), loneliness, terror, and hope, and a stress on the need to be "authentic" or genuine, not drifting with the crowd, in facing up to life and death, in personal choice. Sartre and Camus were atheists, Heidegger a "wavering" agnostic. Other existentialists have been believers in God, like the Jewish Martin Buber (1965) and the convert to Catholicism Gabriel Marcel (d. 1973). Among phenomenological and personalist thinkers who were or are Catholics one can mention St. Edith Stein (a Jewish philosopher of the first rank, who converted to Catholicism, became a Carmelite nun, and was gassed in Aushwitz in 1942) and Karol Wojtyla (the Polish philosopher who combined Aquinas's thought with twentieth-century trends in such works as *The Acting Person* and who eventually became Pope John Paul II; d. 2005).

In the last thirty years or so other developments have occurred in continental philosophy with the rise of what is known as postmodernism and deconstruction. Here, the famous names are Michel Foucault and Jacques Derrida (mentioned above). There has also been much greater interchange and coming together between Anglo-American philosophy and continental thought through the writings of people like Richard Rorty (d. 2007), Charles Taylor, and the Catholic convert Alasdair MacIntyre in North America, and Jürgen Habermas and Paul Ricoeur (d. 2005) in Germany and France. Much in postmodernism and deconstruction appears to be a rehash of subjectivism and relativism. But there are also positive and helpful elements: such analyses help to reveal how our language takes on words with value judgments of which we may not be fully aware. Some of the critiques of contemporary culture and the whole modern period (understood, on this view, as running from the end of the Middle Ages to our own time) offered by postmodernism, especially when handled by writers such as MacIntyre, help us to see that much of the eighteenth-century prejudice against religion and tradition that has filtered down to mass level through mass education and communications is itself suspect and biased.

The position we argued for in cognitional theory would not, perhaps, have been viewed favorably by previous generations of philosophers in the Anglo-American tradition. The logical positivists, who were influenced by Wittgenstein's first phase, objected to philosophical investigations into consciousness. For them science and the logic that science requires to elaborate its theories were the ideal, and philosophy should be seen as simply serving that ideal in some way. Of course their epsitemology is fundamentally empiricist, and therefore the idea of mental acts, of intentional consciousness, would be dismissed as unavailable to scientific theory and thus "mystical"; talk of them would, on this view, lead philosophy astray again. The second phase of Wittgenstein's career, while it marked a radical move away from the logical-positivist vision, was no less unfavorable to philosophy, focusing on consciousness and mental acts. Such philosophical analysis was seen this time as falling foul of ordinary language, which alone is meaningful. The problem for this view is that it is a philosophical position that only ordinary language is meaningful, not an ordinary language one. Positions like that of the late Wittgenstein involve all kinds of analyses of ordinary language that are clearly philosophical. But then one cannot strictly observe that only ordinary language, not philosophy, is meaningful, because that would disqualify itself as a meaningless view. You could not say it, nor coherently think it—so it's false. Analytical philosophers, however, have now moved away from these phases of Anglo-American philosophy, and the philosophy of mind is once again a thriving area of philosophy in this tradition.

In this survery you have encountered rather a lot of names and philosophical traditions. The hope is that you will branch out and begin to read more about these thinkers and the various philosophical traditions they represent. The history of philosophy does not occur in a vaccuum. The study of philosophy's history will also involve you in the wider study of cultural history of which it is a part. Such study of the interaction of philosophy with other aspects of cultural life is a fascinating topic. What has been presented above is also a thematic sketch, a sketch that is part of the argument for the importance of the critical-realist view of Lonergan to which you have been introduced. As was said in chapter 1, philosophy is a conversation across time. It is also a debate across time. In the process of self-discovery, self-appropriation, one involves oneself in that discusion and debate across history. It is important, then, to see how the position that we have argued for, and that you have been invited to check out in your own conscious ex-perience, both emerges from the history of the philosophical conversation and helps you engage in that conversation.

*Chapter 5*

# Metaphysics: What Philosophy Can Tell Us about Reality

## Introduction

"Metaphysics" is probably an even stranger-sounding word to you than "epistemology." You may have heard uses of it in the context of weird New Age cult beliefs or come across it when browsing at those shelves in general bookshops where they put books on UFOs, things that go bump in the night, and so on. You may also have gotten the sense from somewhere that "metaphysical" beliefs are the kind of ideas that people had about the world before science came along and told us what it was all really like. Indeed, in our brief summary of the history of philosophy, we noted how, at the beginning of philosophy, what we might now distinguish as science and metaphysics were not so distinguished.

As we shall see in our section below on science and metaphysics, however, the question of their interrelation is still very much with us. Metaphysics is not a collection of superstitions or deep spiritual wisdom of the ancients depending on your estimation of the importance of science. It is, in fact, when rightly understood, *a body of knowledge made explicit, which is in some way implicit in scientific practice itself*. Aristotle was a thinker interested in every aspect of the universe around him. He was fascinated by the world of biology and the world of physics. The term "metaphysics" comes to us from the fact that its subject matter was treated by Aristotle in a book that came after his works on physics. Thus, from the Greek "physics" and "meta" ("after" or "beyond") we get the word "metaphysics" ("after the book on physics"). Another way of characterizing metaphysics is to say that it is *an attempt to characterize some very general structures of reality.* But before we look at the relationship between science and metaphysics, and some of the elements of metaphysics, we will look at the intimate connection between epistemology and metaphysics.

## Epistemology and Metaphysics: A Hand-and-Glove Fit

We have seen in chapter 2 how one can argue for a view of knowing involving three interrelated levels of mental activities or operations. We also saw that to argue against this account is to find evidence for the truth of the account in the very conscious activities we must use to deny it or question it. Furthermore, attempts to deny that we know reality, or what is the case, are similarly self-destructive, once it is realized that one is claiming, in these very attempts, to know what is so. For again, one can notice that in so arguing, acts of questioning, understanding, judging, and so forth are really and truly going on, and the denial "I know nothing" is really and truly a mental act, a judgment, of a particular kind that one makes.

That was the way we argued, following Lonergan, for a view on human knowing and for objectivity in human knowing, a view that can always be improved but not radically revised, because you would be using it in the revision. But notice something implicit in all of this: if reality, "what is so," "being," is to be known by attention to data, intelligent insight into data, and judgment regarding the insight, then that tells us something not just about knowing but about reality itself. We can say, then, that *reality is what is to be known through the use of our intelligent and reasonable operations; it is what is to be known by intelligent grasp and reasonable judgment.*

We can observe at once a number of important points regarding this. First, what we have given here is what Lonergan terms a "heuristic definition." A "heuristic" concept or definition is one that contains some information about something, perhaps not very much at first, but points us in the direction of further discovery. An illustration is in algebra: we are told something about an $x$, perhaps not much at first, but we are pointed in the direction of further discovery by working with what we are given in the initial equation on this $x$. Second, the heuristic notion of being, or reality, as "that which is to be known by intelligence and reasonableness," is not totally empty. It is quite something, when you think about it, when we say, "That can't be true because its opposite is true" or "That is true because there is sufficient reason to say it's true." What we are saying in these cases is that we somehow *know in advance* that if there is sufficient reason to say something is true, then it is true or real, or if there is sufficient reason to say it is false, then that will be so. In fact, the very attempt to argue that we do not have the capacity to know in advance in this way will only show that we do. Because the debater of the point will try to show that the position just stated is not so, because there is not sufficient reason to say that it is. Inherent in our cognitional activities, in our mental operations, is an ability to rule in and rule out certain things as being real and other things as unintelligible, unreal. This really brings us back to the beginning of philosophy, when Plato wondered at this amazing capacity of human beings to know or recognize the truth when they get to it.

But does this not mean that we cut reality down to our size in some objectionable way? In answer, we have to realize that our ability to in some sense anticipate reality as the intelligible and reasonable is pretty general. We shall see in later sections how we can identify a number of other general features of reality, but even then this only gives us the lightest X-ray shot of the complexity that creation has, or that a creation could have. Further, when we come to the question of God we can say that, yes, indeed, God is still the intelligible—if God were not, he would be absurd. And since the absurd also includes the unintelligible that we call "evil," God would not be the Good; God would not be God. We are faced with an utter mystery in the face of God, however, because, as we shall see, we never encounter in the world a being whose very nature, or essence, is to Be, as is the case with God.

In short, while saying that reality, being, must be in some sense "commensurate" to our knowing, that it is the intelligible and the reasonable, we are saying that this does not pin down in a totally identified way the way things are. If, however, we doubt or deny that reality is the intelligible and reasonable, we will be back with a self-destructive position. For we will be arguing using our intelligence and reason in order to prove something about reality, about the reality, perhaps, of our knowing and its limitations and so forth. There is then something of a hand-and-glove relation of fit between our knowing and the most general characteristics of being or reality. Just as the stomach anticipates some of the general features of what will satisfy its orientation to material, food, that nourishes us, so our minds anticipate features of reality in such a way that they have the capacity to recognize truth and reality when they are found. This is the point of the scholastic (medieval) saying: *lex mentis lex entis* ("the law of the mind is the law of being").

After a brief look at the relationship between metaphysics and science, we will turn, in further sections, to look at other elements in a metaphysical account of reality, a general account of reality. These other elements will unpack a bit further what we can say of this general structure. But throughout these discussions it will be important to note the way in which we link metaphysics back to the work we did on epistemology. In epistemology we affirmed that we are selves, selves who are, among other things, "knowers" who operate on three interrelated levels in coming to know. In our account of the metaphysical elements of the universe, of "pairs of twins," we will relate our earlier discussions of what we can affirm of ourselves as conscious knowers to the discussions of these other general aspects of reality.

## Metaphysics and Science

We said in the introduction that sometimes the word "metaphysics" suggests something prescientific or even occult or antiscientific. When properly understood, however, it implies none of these things. It is, rather, something that is implied in scientific practice and does take us in some ways "beyond" scientific knowledge.

In the middle of the last century, the philosophical school of *logical positivism* became quite influential in English-speaking philosophical circles. Thinkers in this group, like the Austrians Rudolf Carnap (who ended up in the United States, d. 1970) and Otto Neurath (d. 1945), developed a philosophy that was empiricist and that wanted to look to science as the sole benchmark of true, objective knowledge. They looked to Wittgenstein's early work on the logic of language and thought that with an empiricist account of knowing, coupled with well-developed logical techniques, they could capture what was good in scientific practice and thus produce an account of sound human knowing. This could then be used to rule out "bad" subjective claims to knowledge, things like ethics, religious knowledge, and metaphysics. The story of the way logical positivism died in Anglo-American philosophy (it was always regarded with contempt in other traditions of philosophy) cannot be told here. Suffice it to say, any theory linked to an empiricist account is eventually going to end up in skepticism and thus deny objectivity to science as much as to any other kind of knowledge. Hume showed us this in the eighteenth century. A great admirer of Newton, Hume wanted to do for human nature what Newton had done for physical nature: reveal its laws once and for all. But Hume ended up with a philosophy so skeptical that it pulled the rug out from under any scientific account of reality. For we cannot get to objective reality if, like Hume, we say that all our knowing consists of is just the noise of sounds, the color of shapes we see, the tastes or smells of other sensations. In other words, we cannot get to reality if we just stop with the first level of human knowing and do not bring in the other two levels.

Logical positivism, then, has fallen out of favor in philosophy as has its account of scientific knowledge. One of the great opponents of logical positivism and one of the great philosophers of science, Karl Popper (another Austrian who ended up teaching at the London School of Economics) drew people's attention much more to the actual history of science as it had developed. One of Popper's key ideas was that a scientific theory, to be scientific, had to, as it were, go out on a limb. It had to say, "Look, if you do such and such experiments and get such and such results, this theory will be proved true; if you don't get these results it will be proved false." Popper was impressed by what he felt Einstein had done in science by working in precisely this way. Popper was unimpressed, however, by the Marxists and the Freudian psychoanalysts who, he felt, were unscientific, because when any apparent objection to their theory came up they just moved the goal posts to somehow include it. Popper called his benchmark of authentic scientific knowledge "falsifiability" to indicate that a good theory should be vulnerable, falsifiable. Interestingly enough Popper was far more positive about the role of metaphysical systems in the development of science. He pointed out that without the matrix of various metaphysical ideas one would not have had Newtonian physics. Popper did not write much on the idea of "metaphysical research programs," but some of his followers and even many of his critics later did. It has now become generally recognized in the philosophy of science, by most parties, that metaphysics plays a crucial role in the development of science.

We can just mention one example here, which, although it is linked to very technical discussions, can be summarized in an accessible way to bring out the point. In his book *Quantum Mechanics and Objectivity* (The Hague: Nijhoff, 1965), Patrick Heelan, whose philosophy is influenced by Lonergan, gives a philosophical appraisal of some of the debates concerning theoretical issues in quantum mechanics. What is interesting to observe is that this book does not give the impression of a philosopher meddling in science. Rather, as Heelan's book and many other writings on quantum mechanics bring out, the theoreticians themselves more or less clearly acknowledge that a good deal of their theorizing involves philosophical elements. Heelan's book brings out the way two of the key figures in the development of quantum mechanics, Werner Heisenberg (d. 1976) and

Niels Bohr (d. 1962), interpreted what they were doing in accord with quite explicit philosophical views. Heisenberg himself went through various philosophical phases in which he was influenced first by Kant, then by Plato. Bohr, with whom Heisenberg disagreed, outlined the famous Copenhagen interpretation of quantum mechanics, which takes up explicit views on knowledge and reality. It is a view that has been rejected or modified by other theoreticians. The point is, then, that even on this what we might call *explicit level*, twentieth-century science has once again involved itself with theoretical issues that are philosophical or metaphysical, certainly in the sense that they are "beyond physics," strictly speaking. For the earlier logical positivist philosophers of science, such involvement of science with philosophy would have appeared as a nightmarish confusion of "occult nonsense" with clear observations and logical deductions—the kind of thing that their image of science suggested it should be all about.

This mixing of science and philosophy on a pretty much *explicit level* (I will draw out the contrast between *explicit* and *implicit* levels of scientific involvement with philosophy below) can be brought out by reflecting on some other recent developments. A book on questions concerning philosophy and science by the Cambridge University philosopher of science Michael Redhead has the significant title *From Physics to Metaphysics* (Cambridge University Press, 1995), a title that brings out the kind of interrelationship we have been talking about and that most philosophers now accept. One of the areas Redhead looks at is the theory of everything (TOE) scientists such as Stephen Hawking, Frank Tippler, and others. By TOE we mean a grand, unified, scientific account of the universe. Although Stephen Hawking is clearly a remarkable and brilliant scientist, we need sometimes to be wary of a silly type of media hype concerning such gifted persons. What I am getting at is that, just as Newton and Einstein were gifted and brilliant, so we can also see them in their historical context as having inevitable limitations to their work—we should not expect anything different of brilliant theorists today. What media hype can do is to cloud the real intellectual and theoretical issues at stake in discussion. What Michael Redhead and other philosopher-scientists, such as Stanley Jaki (d. 2009), draw attention to is that there are interesting theoretical problems with the very idea of a scientific "grand theory of everything."

The questions are concerning the fundamental notions of such theories. There is nothing wrong, and everything right, with the hope that a scientist will come up with a satisfying theory that accounts for the physical structure of the universe and its behavior. But philosopher-scientists like Redhead and

Jaki provide the useful service of clarifying where and how the scientist may have made the slip of claiming too much for his or her theory. There are a number of very technical difficulties with the idea of a TOE literally giving us a final and definite account of the universe that concerns such matters as Kurt Gödel's (d. 1978) proofs in mathematics. But a point that can be grasped much more easily, and a point that is useful for us to examine, has to do with the ongoing revisability of science. But to be blunt, as Redhead puts it, if we did have a TOE, we would never know finally if it were proved, definitely true, of the universe.

This point has been realized more clearly over the last four hundred years as science has developed: modern science can give us new theories that are probably more true than the older ones, but it cannot finally establish a theory. So the theory of oxygen replaced older theories of phlogiston, because the oxygen theory explained more, explained things more simply, and so forth. We take it that the fact we can build space rockets and get them to fly tends to confirm the accounts of physics that stand behind the technical productions. In a sense, what we have in these cases are "flying experiments"; they are experiments that tend to confirm the theories as do successful experiments in the lab. But what theoreticians and philosophers of science have come to realize more and more clearly, also through a study of the history of science, is that we reach here not definite judgments but probable judgments with regard to our theories being true to reality. There could be a future theory that would do as much and more as our present theory of oxygen and that would thus replace it. We just don't know if scientific revision would ever stop. And TOEs are in the same boat as any other scientific theory.

What we can notice here, however, is that what is more basic than any particular theory or any particular scientific method is actually the method by which we constantly revise theories. And that "method" is our own attention to data, inquiry and insight into data, and reasonable judgment regarding our theory: *in other words, what scientific method depends on is our own operations in cognitional structure*. At this point, then, we reach what we can call the deeper or more *implicit* level of the relationship between philosophy and science. And this brings home to us that what is fundamental is not some particular scientific stage of development of one period but the very intelligent and reasonable operations by which human beings erected science and our departments of inquiry to begin with.

This is not to be subjectivistic about science. On the contrary, our arguments against Kant, idealists, and skeptics in the last chapter lead to a defense of the human capacity to know reality. Further, we can say that if through attention, intelligence, and reasonableness we make a probable judgment that this scientific theory is better than another, on our cognitional structure position, this means that we are right to claim that we have a theory that is probably true of reality. We are not in the position of verifying in the way we are when we verify cognitional theory itself. We can reach definite judgments in that area. So, if I judge that "I do not judge," I can notice in the conscious data that I do actually judge here. It is not the same if I doubt that, say, this discoloration in the test tube is due to theory *x* rather than theory *y*. It is not that in the very process of arguing against or doubting theory *x* I find that theory *x* is actually given in the data of my own consciousness. No, scientific investigation is like detective work: inferences are made on the basis of data. But the correct theory is never known to be definitely given. In this detective story only God has actually seen the "crime," the actual cause of the data. Still, one can say that probable judgments are possible, and one theory is preferred as being more likely to be true of reality than another.

To bring out this deeper interconnection between science and philosophy and, more precisely, metaphysics, we can point out further that science, just as any other human inquiry, gets going and moves along because of that native capacity we have to anticipate reality in our questions and answers, in our seeking to know being, by operating on the three levels of cognitional structure. So implicit in all science, as a particular kind of inquiry, is the anticipation of reality or being as the intelligible and reasonable, as that which is to be known through the use of intelligence and reason. *Implicit in all science is what we have brought out as a metaphysics of being as the intelligent and reasonable.*

Finally, in this section, we can say a few words on the relationship between scientific and commonsense knowing. With the rise of modern science it often seemed that what people had claimed to know about the real world was shown not to be so: the world now seemed a strange and unfamiliar place. "What goes up must come down," people had said, but with space flight that does not hold true. We can note, in passing, that ironic as it may seem, the rise of modern science has a profoundly spiritual aspect to it. While in most cultures people have coupled a commonsense way of knowing the world with a belief in a spiritual world, still one can see how easily empiricism and materialism can progress if one just has a commonsense knowledge of things: "Here are real things, with size, color, shape, etc. That's all there is to reality." But modern science implies that reality is more than we can simply know through the use of our senses—it makes it difficult for empiricists to say, "That's all there is."

Sir Arthur Eddington (d. 1944) put the new difficulty of the relationship between ordinary knowing and scientific knowing in the form of a little scientific parable. He said, "Here is my table. From the commonsense view, it is a solid, brown, continuous surface surmounted on four solid, brown legs. But from the viewpoint of science? Well, it is mostly empty space, with now and again something in it that can be described as a particle or as a wave." The dilemma can come when we ask the question, "Which is the real table?" And some people have been led to say that commonsense knowledge is not knowledge at all but illusion, while others, even theorists like Bohr, have gone in the other direction: reality is table and chairs. The strange elements of the world of physics, in this view, are a kind of "useful fiction."

But from the viewpoint of cognitional theory we can say that neither of these paths is to be taken. Science grows out of common sense and returns to it to modify its views with the products and ways of new technical procedures. Furthermore, the commonsense judgment that there is a table here is just as much a matter of intelligence and reasonableness as is the scientific account. You and I agree (level of intelligence) on what we mean by the word "table," and it is a matter of reasonable judgment to decide whether there is one of these things in the room upstairs or not. We need to verify our judgments by going up there and looking. Science simply asks further questions and is interested in things in a different way than I am in my ordinary concerns. Both the scientist and the layperson can make the commonsense judgment as to whether the stuff in the test tube is turning green or is turning red; the scientist has, of course, other concerns and interests in doing so. But both of them can be or can fail to be objective about that simple judgment, and without making thousands of other such simple judgments throughout his research career the scientist would never get going in science.

## Metaphysical Terms: Sets of Twins

In looking at our "sets of twins" we will observe the meaning of some metaphysical terms, terms characterizing something of reality, as these occur in the classical philosophy of Aristotle, St. Thomas, and others. We will then briefly relate each set to our discussion of cognitional structure, bringing out the intimate interconnection between epistemology and metaphysics.

### Existence and Essence

In so many ways the pairs of metaphysical twins we are looking at in these sections are very obviously implied in all our language and thought about the world, in our scientific, scholarly language as much as in everyday language. One of the things we are up to here, then, is simply to draw these items, of which we have always in some way been conscious, into the light for a closer inspection. So, ever since we were small children we have been aware of the distinction in reality between existence and essence. For the distinction is simply between *what a thing is* and *that a thing is*. We can immediately relate this to our discussion of cognitional structure: on the level of intelligence we ask, "What is that?" about some data, and we want to have some idea, insight, understanding. But, as we have said, there are further questions once we have had our bright idea: "Is it just a bright idea? Does it actually exist?" So the real things in the world, which correspond to our knowing, have at least these two elements to them: *they have a nature*, an *essence*, *"a what,"* and if they are real, they also have *existence*; we say they *actually exist*. So a lion, a democracy, Fred Jones, or a neutrino all have natures: they are things we understand; they could not be as they are had they not these selfsame natures. But beyond that, if they exist, they have quite literally something more: they have existence.

Again, returning to cognitional structure, we can bring out the significance of this difference further. When we have the idea or concept of a nature (on the second level) of Fred, or a battle, or a price rise in beetroot, or a cat, we have not thereby come to know that any of these things actually exist. We need to "know more"; literally, we need to know by grasping in an act of judgment that these natures actually exist. Think of cognitional structure itself: you had to go through the difficult and demanding process of trying to grasp something of what was meant by the structure, by the three levels, the consciousness we have in them, and so forth; that was grasping an essence, a nature. But that did not settle things as regards reality, as regards the actual existence of that structure of knowing. You had to try to verify that in your own conscious experience by, among other things, trying to doubt it.

Scientific practice, again, is committed to anticipating this metaphysical structure in reality. For we can say that *a scientific theory is a theory verified in instances*. As theory, it is an understanding of a nature or essence; as verification, it is a knowledge that this essence, of a tropical spider, a photon, or whatever, actually exists. Our use of the word "actual" is not incidental here. St. Thomas speaks in terms of the "act of existence." It may seem a bit odd to talk of existence as an act, but as the language I have been using so far indicates, we do point this way when we talk of something "actually existing."

There is an important point here for philosophical reflection on God. St. Thomas argues against the ontological argument. That is the argument that says we can prove the existence of God simply from knowing his essence: we can know existence from essence. St. Thomas disagrees and says that for human knowing we always have a further question when we have grasped an essence or a nature of something: does this thing actually exist? St. Thomas, however, does grant that if one did know God's nature, as only God does, one would know that, given this nature, God must exist. Because, St. Thomas argues, God alone is the One whose very nature it is to exist. Every other being is a creature, and creatures are *contingent*, not *necessary* (another pair of metaphysical twins). A contingent thing is one that might exist or might not exist. All the natures or essences we come across or could think up are like that: I can think of a dodo, a rabbit, a person's emotions, but just by thinking of them I do not know if they exist. They are the kinds of things that *might exist* or *might not exist*: they are contingent. Something that exists necessarily would be a being who, when you understood his nature, you would also know (in a sense you would also at once judge) that he is.

Finally, we can make a further subdivision in the category of existence. This subdivision links up with the rather strangely named metaphysical twins we will be discussing below named "substances and accidents." What we can note for the present is this: we have said that if we know Uncle John, the cat, and the atom all exist, then we know (a) a certain nature, essence, and (b) that this essence actually exists. So we have talked of the *act of existence of a thing*. But notice that we cannot only talk of the act of existence of a thing or person like a human being, an animal, or an atom, but also the act of existence (the actual existence) of an event: of John's lifting the cup, of John's making a judgment, of the cat jumping on the table, or of the atom spinning. These things we usually call "occurrences." Again, they have "essences"; we understand on level 2 what it is to raise a cup, have a thought, jump up, and so forth, and similarly we also need to know if these essences are actually realized. We do that in a judgment about what has actually happened (level 3). But clearly, the "act of existence" of a whole person, or of a thing or creature, is somewhat different from all the real occurrences these things or persons go through of, say, jumping, spinning, running, or thinking. So using the terms *act of existence* and *act of occurrence* can be a convenient way of distinguishing these two types of existence that we encounter in reality.

### Form and Matter

You may recall that in our whistle-stop tour of philosophy we mentioned that Plato had the view that in meeting the data of experience we came to knowledge by "remembering" forms or exemplars of things. We then discovered representatives of these ideal types in the real world; Aristotle rejected this and held that we really discover the forms or ideas of things in the data of our experience of the world—we do not simply remember them. But Aristotle retained the distinction between matter and form as an essential part of metaphysics. This hylemorphic position ("hyle" the Greek indicating "matter" and "morphic" from the Greek "morphe" or "form") has played some kind of role in most metaphysical views since then.

What we are on to here is not some kind of antiquated Greek scientific view (as we are with the view of the four "humors"), rather this is again a metaphysical distinction regarding reality that is always operative in any scientific practice. The word "matter" is, like a number of these terms, a bit misleading in this regard: it suggests some kind of physics of the very basic "stuff" or particles. But the form/matter distinction is not really about that kind of up-front scientific subject at all.

What does it indicate then? *The "form" is the idea or concept of something; "matter" indicates the particular instantiations of the same kind of things.* Many, many things can have the same "form." Many Ford Escorts roll off the production line; there are many instances of human beings throughout the planet; there are many more instances of atoms or neutrinos throughout the universe. We can say that each thing is both "alike" and yet is not the selfsame thing. How? Why? Because all the Fords or atoms, insofar as they are similar, have the same form or idea; but they are different insofar as each is a different material realization of the same idea or blueprint. When two pins are in all respects identical in form, they are still not the same thing. Why? We say there is merely a *material difference* between them; the same form "pin" is empirically or materially *instantiated* ("instanced") in two individuals. This is what we mean by talking of the "matter" of a thing. We are simply referring, by this term, to the difference between "that one there" and "this one here."

It is not what science means by the term "matter." In contemporary science that has a definite description, a definite form. This chair has the same form as that one over there: the design of both is "postwar classroom utility." But their "matter" is different; that piece of wood over there is not this piece of wood over here. But then the wood of either chair is itself a further example of form/matter reality. For the type of wood is something understood by grasping an idea or form of "cherry," "beech," or "larch," and so on down through the biological and chemical makeup of the wood: one is coming to chemical compounds of such and such a type, and the form/matter distinction does not stop but just recurs, because this chemical compound is of the same type as that. But what makes them different then? Merely their material instantiation—the difference involves "matter" in the metaphysical sense. Whatever the ultimate particles are in the physical world, however far down they discover new particles, one will never arrive at "matter" in the metaphysical sense we mean here. Why not? Because whatever these particles are, if there is still more than one of them then this "tinkytonk" (or whatever the name they give them) here will have the same form but will be a different individual from that "tinkytonk" there; and the difference will be merely *material*.

Scientific practice works with this distinction as does all our human knowing. In our knowing, on the second level of knowing, we have insights into or about the data we encounter. In an insight we grasp a form, or idea. But in doing so we "abstract" the form from its particular material circumstances. When a scientist understands the molecular structure of water or the biological structure of the tuna fish, he or she moves from individual cases to the general. We do not have a different physics for Birmingham and one for Newcastle. Rather, the scientist grasps forms in the data and leaves aside what is irrelevant to understanding these forms or ideas that have to do with their particular space-time location. Think of this in mathematics: One can have the definition of a circle. But it is irrelevant to the definition, to grasping the form of what makes a circle circular, to say that this one was drawn in pencil, that one in chalk, etc. And, if one is just thinking of circularity in general without thinking of circles of particular sizes, then in grasping the form "circle," one is abstracting from all the dimensions of any particular circles in reality. But while we can abstract in understanding a form from any particular material instance, while we can understand "cat," "atom," "composer," "friend," abstracting from what is peculiar to any particular one of these, there still cannot be any of these things without a particular realization of them; and the particular realization of each one is what we refer to when we talk of their *material* or *empirical* difference, one from another.

### Potency and Act

We talk of someone having "great potential," and we are glad when such a person realizes it, or "actualizes" it. The distinction between potency and act draws our attention to such distinctions in reality. Potency can be distinguished from mere abstract possibility. It is possible that this car never existed; it is a contingent being. It can exist, but it does not have to; it would be possible for it to not exist. It is possible that in another world trees could be all blue, and so on. But we are talking of a different kind of possibility when we say that a famous pianist has the "potential" to play a piano concerto. He is not *actually* playing it because he is, say, asleep, but he *could* do so; he has the potential to do so when he awakes in the way that I do not, for I don't have that skill. When he starts playing we can say the potency to play the piano comes to *act*. The acorn is the oak in potency; when it grows it will be the oak in act.

We can make some further distinctions here. I do not have the potency, potential, to play the piano as does the pianist. But I do, really, have the potential to play the piano in the way a rat or a stone does not. What, in that case, is the difference between the pianist and me? Well, his potential is nearer to a possible realization because he has the *habitus*, Aristotle and Aquinas would say, the habit of playing, which he does not lose in sleep. A further point: you may have wondered about the connection between "act" in this section and "act of existence" and "act of occurrence" discussed above. Yes, they are referring to the same thing. The pianist exists—he actually exists (act of existence)—and when he plays the piano, utilizing his habit, his potential becomes realized in various acts of occurrence: moving fingers, understanding notes, phrases, etc.

### Substance and Accidents

"The chemist knocked the bottle with the substance in it onto the floor and said to his assistant, 'Accidents will happen.'" Yes, that is rather the kind of picture that comes to mind when we meet this pair of metaphysical twins. But again, we have to understand by the terms "substance" and "accidents" something rather different from what is suggested by our chemist story, and perhaps finding alternative expressions for the terms will also help to elucidate their meaning.

By "substance" in metaphysics we mean a unity or an identity or, perhaps, a thing. What are we referring to here? Well, we mean the kinds of things that we indicate by nouns: persons, animals, atoms, angels, God. By such "identities" we mean not just a bundle of things but a functional, active unity. We can point to a heap of stones and say to a friend, "There is one over there." One what? Well, heap of stones. But we do not think of a heap of stones or pile of bricks as being "one," as being a real "unity," as we do a lion or a person or a tree.

If unities or identities like trees, animals, or persons are indicated by nouns in our language, verbs often indicate what we mean by "accidents," or (another translation of Aristotle's term) "differentiae." For "accidents" indicate all the changes, both active and passive, through which such individuals go. Thus the same man can be now happy and now sad, and now a mixture of both; the same tree can look one color at dawn, another at sunset, can whither or grow strong, can be moved to another location. The notions of substance and accidents are then complimentary. We think of the same identity as going through many changes but remaining the same.

There are philosophical questions and problems that arise in this area, often emerging from one's view of knowledge. To notice how such problems in metaphysics emerge from one's epistemology is a good exercise in realizing the intimate interconnection between the two areas in philosophy. So David Hume, who as we saw in our history section above, pushed empiricism to its logically skeptical conclusion, saw a difficulty in claiming that we really know the existence of unities or identities in reality. All we have in knowledge, in Hume's view, is the stuff from level 1 (as we, not Hume, would call it). We have the colors, sights, smells, and so on, of sensation. We just have the accidents, one might say. We don't know, we are not given in experience, the unities that go through all these changes. This skepticism applies also to myself, in Hume's view. Given Hume's very passive account of human knowing, he ends up by saying that when I look within myself, I do not find an "I," a self, a substance that goes through many changes, but simply impressions and sensations. All I find when I "look within," says Hume, "is a bundle of fleeting perceptions."

As I wish to bring in Hume again in our section below on *cause*, it might be as well to say a few words on his view of human knowing here and to identify where the problems occur in it. We can then contrast his view with cognitional structure and see how these views have differing implications for such metaphysical notions as substance.

We can identify virtually a one, two, three pattern in Hume's account of knowing. On a first level are all the experiences of sensation, of the five senses, and also "inner feelings" of anger, love, and so forth. On level 2, for Hume what we have are our ideas. But what are they? Quite literally they are dull afterimages of our sensations. So I see the sights of a brightly colored room, then I close my eyes and still see duller shapes of these things. That is all that an idea is for Hume—a faint mental picture. Then, according to what is essential in his account, we have the mental "glue" between these ideas. And the mental association between our ideas is simply *custom* and *habit*. We get into the habit of expecting certain things to happen in the world, and so we say they must happen, they are caused to happen. But all this is just because of our long, habitual training—like the rat on the wheel that expects the cheese of the experimenter to fall after ten turns of the wheel. Finally, as what we could identify as a level 3, Hume has an account of *belief*, an account of the genesis of our beliefs. Here Hume distinguishes between when we believe something is so and when we simply think it fiction, as we do in distinguishing between a fairy story, say, and an account in a letter of a friend. But the crux is that all belief is, again, for Hume, just something we get stuck with, nonrationally, subrationally, because of constant training or habit.

Hume is a fascinating thinker, but one might say that, in the end, his strength is to have tried to push empiricism as far as it will go, and all kinds of cracks and strains start to show in his work. We shall look at some of these on cause below. But we can notice here some problems. For one thing, Hume's account of the genesis and change of beliefs, we should say judgments, does not fit with his own practice. That is, he wants to claim that the establishment of all human beliefs is like rat-on-the-wheel training and is irrational. *But the way he tries to change our old beliefs in this and establish the new Humean beliefs does not square with his own account, for he attempts to change our beliefs through intelligent and reasonable argument.* In other words we have here an example of applying the work of a thinker to itself to see where it has self-destructive elements.

Our main concern here, however, is to see the connection between Hume's account of knowing and his account of the self. What happens is that, in Hume's view, everything in our knowing is a sort of passive reception of sense data coupled with a "glue" between mental pictures that is just imposed irrationally. But this does not square with the intelligence and reasonableness Hume used, or anyone else studying his account has to use, in order to argue for the view. There is an oversight particularly of the levels of intelligence and reasonableness in coming to know. But when one does come to affirm these levels, one also comes to affirm, as we have done in chapter 2, that in one's knowing one is a dynamic, self-assembling structure of interrelated mental acts operating on three levels. One is claiming to know something of the self in claiming to know one's knowing. And that is a real self, a unity, that remains the same through the various conscious acts of attending to data, questioning, insight, further question, judgment, and so on. It is the same one consciousness in all of this. For if I am to make a judgment I need to make it about something I have understood and about data I have experienced. If I look out of the window and say, "Yes, the milkman has come," I am aware not only of an act of conscious judgment but also of acts of attention to data and of answering a question I have asked. All these acts have to be present in the one consciousness that I am in order for the judgment to occur. But this oneness is not merely passive. As we have noted in chapter 2, the oneness of myself as a unity, a substance, is also a dynamic oneness that gets things going, that wants to know, that wills to pay attention to data, and drives on with further questions.

On the cognitional structure account of knowing, then, we can identify in our own case a *substance*, a unity, that goes through many different *accidents*, or occurrences of acts, of mental "doings," in the very process of coming to know. Hume's "passive bundle" is an oversight of the very activities he has to use to make his argument and of the dynamic unity of the one consciousness he, or anyone thinking about his account, is.

### Types of Cause

In every type of discourse, ordinary conversation, science, engineering, musicology, history, psychology, or literary study, we use words such as "why" and "because." If we break that latter word up into "be" and "cause" we shall notice that we are talking about the causes of things in the world constantly: the cause of that election result, of my friend's reaction, of the computer malfunction, of this chemical reaction, and so on. Philosophy, in the area of metaphysics, tries to bring this idea of cause into the light and examine it explicitly.

If we turn to Aristotle, Plato, and Aquinas we can notice a number of types of causes being distinguished: (internal causes) material cause, formal cause; (external causes) efficient cause, exemplary cause, final cause. Let us look at each of these in turn, bearing in mind all the time that a cause is really a "because," an explanation of why something is such and such.

*Internal causes: Material cause and formal cause.* We can distinguish between the causes internal to a being and those external to it. When we talk of material and formal causes of something, clearly we are referring to the distinction between matter and form we made above. But why talk of these as causes? Well remember, a cause is something we get to know as a "because" in answer to a question, "why?" So if I ask, "Why is this lump of wood in this shape?" I can answer that it is made like that because it is made up as a chair, something human beings sit on. The formal cause, the "why" of "why" this thing is as it is, is the form of chair imposed on the matter by the carpenter. And clearly you cannot have a chair without the matter. "Why are there no chairs in your workshop?" "Be*cause* we ran out of wood." The material cause of why we have a chair here is the necessary wood.

Since the rise of modern science, there has been much debate about what kind of causes modern science tries to discover. Many argue that it is not concerned with final causes. But when one thinks about it, what it clearly is concerned with is discovering the formal cause. Aristotle put things this way: when I ask, "Why are these flesh and bones a man?" or "Why are these bits of wood, glass, and bricks arranged in this way?" (when I am looking at a house) what I am after is the formal cause. That is, I want to understand why the data appear to me as they do, why they are arranged or patterned before me as they are. So when I understand the form of "man" or "house," I understand why things are such and such rather than another way. This is what the scientist is after in trying to understand why the data in his test tube or wherever appear as they do.

*External causes: Efficient cause, final cause, and exemplary cause.* What we mean by these causes, which are needed to bring a being into existence, can be illustrated with the example of a bridge. The efficient cause of the bridge across the river is the actual work, activity, of putting the structures in place—the human exertion, the work of machines. The final cause is the "end" or purpose for which all this activity is expended: the value of making a new, wider bridge for traffic at this point. The exemplary cause would be the plan conceived in the mind or minds of the engineers and designers according to which the work is realized.

Notice the way this discussion of causes relates to our earlier treatment of essence and existence. The essence or idea of "bridge" is not something that by thinking about it we know it is the case in the real world. Its *existence* is *contingent*: it could be or not be. Therefore, for it to be, it must be brought into being by causes external to it. This is the kind of reasoning that we can extend to argue for the existence of God.

We said above that we would look again at Hume in this section. We saw in the section on substance and accidents how Hume's philosophy challenged the idea that we could have reasonably established beliefs about the real nature of the world, for all we have is "perceptions," sense impressions. Further, our ideas about the world as having real structures to it come about simply as irrational habits. The prime example here is the case of causation, or causes in the real world. We see one billiard ball hit another and the second move off at speed but we don't see the cause. We don't know if tomorrow the second ball will just disappear into thin air or will go backward into the other one. All our expectations and anticipations are merely the result of habit and custom: we keep seeing the same things happening, one after the other, so we get into the habit of saying one thing is caused by the other. But we don't really know this. The upshot is that we do not know if there is real cause and effect in the world. There is a fallacy, a mistake, in logical thinking called *post hoc, ergo propter hoc* (after this, therefore because of this). We can say that for Hume the whole human race is trapped in such a fallacy by its habits. Such habits are no more rational than is the expectation of the rat in the experimenter's cage that gets into the habit of expecting cheese to fall after ten turns of the running wheel. We human rats think that the ten turns *cause* the fall of cheese, but really this is not so, for tomorrow the experimenter could drop no cheese at all.

We have seen in the last section, however, how problems arise in Hume's account. One of the strains in the position is that Hume wishes to do for human nature what Newton had done for physical nature—discover its laws and explain its behavior. But if, in Hume's view, we cannot discover causes in the real world, then science is finished. But it gets worse. Hume actually tells us (and uses the forbidden word) that he has shown the *cause* of why we make the mental associations we do about the world: it is due to the effects of habit and custom. *He therefore tries to give an explanation of our behavior, give some causes of our behavior, while denying that any human investigator can rationally establish causes and explanations.* This is linked to the criticism we noted in the previous section: Hume uses intelligence and reason to attempt to change our beliefs about our knowing while denying that human beliefs are brought into being or changed reasonably.

If we turn again here to our work on epistemology, cognitional structure, we can again relate to it our discussions of cause in order to bring home the connections between metaphysics and epistemology. Is it true, as Hume maintains, that we have no direct experience of cause in reality? Hume pursues his point in the direction we will go, but, given his "passive" account of human knowing, it is not surprising that he does not quite get to where he should. In the *Enquiry concerning Human Understanding*, he argues that we do not have direct experience of cause and effect, even in our mental life. For, he says, if one were to will that the picture of one's house come into one's mind and then find that it did, one would still not *see* the causal connection between willing and "house picture." God, or some other cause, might have popped the image into one's mind just at the point one wanted it.

If, however, we reflect on what we have looked at in cognitional structure, we can see that in the area of our own conscious operations in coming to know we *are aware* of causal interactions. If I make the judgment that there is a car outside, I am aware of doing so because I hear the sounds, see the sights, or smell the odors. I am directly aware of the reasonableness of my (probable) judgment *because* of the presence of the evidence. I am aware of saying there is a car outside *because* of the evidence, and I am aware precisely of this causal or "because" relationship, *for I am aware of saying this because I experience that*. I am also aware of trying to struggle with this passage or follow through Hume's little thought experiment *because* I want to, *because* I see a value in doing so; my act occurs consciously and consciously aware of the cause or value of doing or pursuing *x*. And the doing or pursing *x* as a value or an "end" is what we refer to as the "final cause" of an action.

Now it is no doubt true that in most cases in which we claim there is a causal relation between one thing and another in the world we cannot be completely certain. Hume is right to a certain degree and to a certain extent. For as we saw above in our section on science, science is a matter of inference similar to detective work. No scientist actually "sees" once and for all the cause. Scientists may see data that are interpreted as supporting a hypothesis that says *x* is the cause of *y*, but the whole history of science and the development of philosophy of science bring home to us that science is a matter of inference from the data to the best available judgment, probable judgment, as to the explanation or cause of whatever data are before us. But what Hume misses is our awareness of intelligible causal relations in our own thought. It is because we are aware of causal intelligibility, of the dependence of one thing on another, that human beings have a capacity to "interrogate the world," put things to the test, to try to find explanations, causal links between things; albeit most of our endeavors arrive at probable judgments as to the causes behind things in the world. Still these judgments are probable and they are established reasonably. So Hume pays little attention to the fact that since the dawn of humanity people have always tinkered with the world to see if there is evidence of some *A* really being the cause of some *B*. Imagine the kind of thing that happens in human history and cultures: the tribesman's clan says that when there is a bad hunt it is because the eagle dance has not been performed properly. But eventually, somehow, this gets put to the test: the dance is not done at all and yet the hunt is bountiful. People have always had the curiosity to try to suppress *A* and see if *B* will still happen or not. And this tinkering with the world, trying to find causal links, is what occurs in a particular way in science, scholarship, and other cognitive disciplines.

### A Developing Universe

Another area in which philosophy (metaphysics) and science can make a mutually conditioning contribution to our understanding of reality is in appreciating something of the overall, developing dynamism of the universe as a whole.

In Aristotle's worldview, a combination of his metaphysical views and scientific views, the place for development was somewhat minimal. The emphasis was more on the recurrent cycles of nature and the continual movement of the stars and celestial bodies. Events on earth were known to deviate from regular and ordered patterns, however, and Aristotle had a place for "chance." His reflections on the phenomenon of "chance" still contain vital and interesting insights. He recognizes, for instance, that chance can play a decisive role in human history, and he writes of our inability to precisely predict the outcome of certain events (he thinks of a sea battle on the morrow, the outcome of which is not predictable). There is also, however, the germ of the idea of development and history in some of Aristotle's thoughts on the way human inquiry into truth is a collective effort in which time and development are crucial.

When we come to Aquinas we find a number of elements in Aristotle's scientific worldview retained. The sense of time, however, is now made different by Aquinas's very context; that is, the Judeao-Christian theology of time as moving on to a climax in history, history as definitively divided before and after the incarnation and moving onward to the climax of a new heaven and earth—salvation history. In Aquinas, then, the image of human persons as creatures in the tension of development, away from sin and into the new life of Christ and his sacraments, becomes pronounced.

The ideas of development, history, dynamic growth, and decline in the universe have, however, been ones that have come more and more to the fore in the last two hundred years. Such developments, then, suggest a metaphysics of development, growth, history. How have some of these ideas themselves developed?

Interestingly enough the great period of scientific advance from the fifteenth to the eighteenth centuries tended, in many ways, to move human thinking away from reflection on development and novelty in the natural world. The great achievements of scientists like Newton gave rise to the eighteenth-century image of the universe as some kind of perpetual-motion clock. Once one discovered all the laws of this mechanism, the universe, one would know how it would tick on endlessly for all eternity. This worldview, developed by thinkers in the Enlightenment period, suggested a determinism that suggested freedom, including human freedom, was out. Rather, the image was of a mechanistic, deterministic world; if you knew enough about the train tracks you could predict forever how the train, the universe, would chug along.

Yet at the very time when this view had seemed to come to dominate, the seeds of its demise were being sown. The great Jesuit scientist of the eighteenth century, Fr. Ruggiero Boscovitch, appears, in his study of physics and Newtonian physics, to have anticipated twentieth-century thinking. That is, he held that Newton's laws only held in the case of large bodies and great distances. On the microscopic level the role of chance variations was back. Gradually, through the nineteenth and into the twentieth century, the role of statistical estimations of developing and declining processes grew in importance in science. Various theories of evolution in the eighteenth and nineteenth centuries contributed here. And as we move into the twentieth century, quantum mechanics again argued with Boscovitch that "classical" or general laws did not totally capture individual microprocesses. In recent years what, perhaps misleadingly, is called "chaos theory" has been celebrated in the media—and we are told that, scientifically, when it gets only a little way down the road, a sheer guess about the weather has as much objective chance of being correct as do the forecasts (we didn't need science to tell us that one). Chaos theory is, in fact, not some one new theory, but rather a drawing together of ways in which in various sciences over the last one hundred years or so probabilistic or statistical analyses have become more and more prominent. Interestingly enough, the use of supercomputers has not brought the prospect of predicting the future in a determinate way any nearer—as some eighteenth-century philosophers thought might be possible. Rather, their programs just confirm the picture. Thus, if two states of affairs, almost identical in structure, start on their paths of development, pretty soon so many factors will have altered their development, one from another, that it will become impossible to predict beyond a limit.

This means that there is a freedom, an unpredictability, even in natural processes, that runs counter to the eighteenth-century philosophies of determinism and mechanism. One thing interesting to understand about such a worldview is that it entails a third category beyond stable process on the one hand and mere chance on the other. In a world of statistical probability, one actually has some understanding of an intelligibility about how likely or not things are to be. Thus we can estimate the chances of someone's winning the lottery, and this estimation will vary if there are fifty numbers on the card, or if there are ten (nice!) or one hundred fifty. We are not talking about sheer chance but about probabilities. Given the potential of things in the universe, the more chances they have to realize these potentials, the more probable the realization will be. There is something of theological significance to grasp here. Sometimes people ask, "Why is the universe so large? Why is it of such an incredible age?" The answer may well be that its time and size are in direct proportion to the right circumstances coming together such that the potential of the universe to realize intelligent life comes to fruition. As the story goes, the more monkeys you have in a room full of typewriters, and the longer you have them there, the greater the likelihood that one will bang out a few words from Shakespeare.

We can relate something of what has been said above on form and matter and potency and act to this area of a developing universe. We saw that in the case of, say, a chair, the reality is the form, chair, and the matter, wood. But we noted that the wood itself is form and matter; wood of this particular kind, "form," realized in all the different instances. What we can note here is that beings on a certain level in the universe can play "matter" to the next level up; they can form the potency from which new creatures develop in their acts of existence and occurrence. So we see this in the emergence of new species of animals, which develop and adapt to exploit some ecological niche. All the creatures in that ecological niche—the plants, the water, other chemical and mineral substances, etc.—are ticking away at what they do; their acts of occurrence (respiration, taking nourishment, excretion, etc.) are going on. Now a species of animal, or perhaps fish, can adapt to exploit and develop the potential of this situation so that their biological acts of living, acts of occurrence, depend on the lower level acts of other creatures: those lower level creatures, with their own natures (form/matter) provide the matter, potency, for the emergence of the higher creatures. Long periods of time and numerous instances, again, increase the statistical likelihood of animals developing in such a way as to exploit this or that particular ecological niche.

### *Spirit and Matter*

We end this chapter on metaphysics by reflecting on whether philosophy can contribute to the human discussion of the destiny of the human person. Is there something spiritual about the human person that could be argued for in philosophical terms, that would suggest that we do not cease to exist at death? What does it mean to talk of "spirit" and "matter"?

The first thing we can say is that philosophically speaking, "matter" is not just a self-evident term. We have seen that in our view of metaphysics we can give a sense to the term "matter," but it did not imply the materialist view that says whatever is real is material. That view is in crisis. In an interview with Bryan Magee, the famous empiricist and philosopher W. V. Quine (d. 2000) remarked that since science now postulates the existence of things we cannot see, taste, or sense in any way, his materialist view now had to be a matter of faith (see Bryan Magee, *Men of Ideas*, BBC Books, 1972). Since the decline of empiricism, then, we cannot boldly affirm that reality is whatever is to be sensed. "Matter," we would have to say, means something intrinsically connected to space and time. Second, you may recall our general designation of the real, of reality, as being "whatever is to be known by intelligent grasp and reasonable affirmation." But that designation does not include the stipulation that everything is material or bound up with the space-time realm inextricably. If we deny the designation we find, as we have repeated often, that we are committed to it: we are arguing intelligently and reasonably that what is to be known is not to be known through intelligence and reason—a self-destructive claim. But is it not self-destructive to argue that not everything is material, is of the space-time empirical domain?

One philosophical or metaphysical view we ought to look at briefly here is *reductionism*. This is the philosophical view, not the scientific view, that all reality is to be reduced to some basic level, or that the levels of reality go so far up, but the rest is mirage or fiction. By this one means that the levels studied by physics, chemistry, biology, sensitive psychology, and then the human sciences are to be collapsed down. So some reductionists say the only truly real is the level of physics—all the rest is a kind of mirage, and physics will explain it all. Behaviorist psychology is a version of reductionism but somewhat different from the previous one. The behaviorist psychologist says that all our beliefs and thoughts are merely the products of some nonrational forces; that is, they can be reduced to or explained by the approach taken to our potty training, or by something similar.

What is wrong with such views of the human person? Well to start with, scientific and scholarly practice do not, in fact, reduce everything to one level. If a physicist is studying subatomic particles it is a matter of indifference to him whether these particles are in a desk, a river, an elephant's trunk, or a person's eye. There are all sorts of other levels of explanation to be brought in as we ascend the ladder of life. This is again connected with the form/matter distinction. It is vital to know the nature of the wood of which a chair is made if you are going to understand the durability of the product. But you have not understood the reality "chair" simply and solely by studying the wood, however minutely you look at it through a microscope. You also need to understand the form "chair." And in understanding the way this chair is as it is you need not only to understand the wood "matter" but also the furniture styles conditioned by a certain culture; you need not only a botanist and a carpenter but the man from the *Antiques Roadshow* as well.

As the philosopher John Searle remarks, you do not understand the behavior of West Coast American cocktail guests simply by understanding physics.

But there is an even deeper objection to reductionism. We can look at it in terms of how behaviorist psychology is mistaken. The behaviorist wants to explain all your beliefs by reducing them to irrational psychological forces—how you were trained. But in doing so he puts forward a scientific hypothesis. What is that? Well, it is something arrived at through the use of cognitional structure, through attention to the data, intelligent insight, questioning, and judgment as to the probable theory. But then to put forward the view that human beliefs have nothing to do with intelligence and reason, that rather they are all established by kinds of potty training or psychological conditioning, is to put forward a self-destructive position. For Professor *X* is claiming his theory is supported by the evidence that his peers can review—not that he is putting forward his theory as an irrational action that is due to bad conditioning. All reductionism, if pushed far enough, then, becomes self-destructive; it saws off the branch on which it is sitting. For if I put forward the view that all my judgments and thought are controlled by "tinkytonks" or "binkybonks" in my brain or wherever, and not by my conscious acts of intelligence and reason, then I disqualify my own hypothesis as something no more reasonable than a cough. Of course my intelligence and reason are conditioned in all sorts of ways by the physical, by my neurological processes. I stop thinking when I am tired; it is hard to think when in pain or delirious. But this is a conditioning of one level by another, rather like the wood for the chair. What I cannot do is deny the reality of the level of my own cognitional acts because, as we have seen all along, the acts of denial will provide evidence in my consciousness that I do come to know in this way. And since any scientific theory, in its inception, development, and revision (brain physiology included), is a product of my conscious intelligence and reason, it cannot deny that intelligence and reason without denying itself.

A further issue we can look at here is the question: Are human minds reproduced in machines? That is to say, is the human mind just a computer? In the sci-fi stories we see that complete replicates of humans will be made in the not-too-distant future. Is this a realistic projection or part of stories that are really modern versions of fairy stories?

A starting point on this question is to observe that at the root of the very mathematics and logic behind the computer are theorems that actually give a no in answer to these questions. The modern computer developed out of the philosophy of logic and mathematics. Computers are devices that speed up

calculation along the paths of special logical structures that human mathematical logicians have drawn up for them. These calculating schemes of
logic are meant to capture the way we proceed logically. But here's the rub.
The very fellows who developed these logical systems came to an impasse.
It is much too technical a story to try to recount here. But people like Kurt
Gödel and Alonzo Church (d. 1995) demonstrated that in the very logical
systems on which the computer is based, there are "undecidability problems." But it gets worse: they also proved that these points in the schemes
are in principle undecidable. What does all this mean? Well, to try to put it
as simply as possible, the logical schemes or systems that either a person
or a computer can follow cannot in principle settle problems you or I with
a moment's reflection can settle. Take the argument:

> Everyone loves someone,
> therefore: Joan loves herself.

Now, with a moment's reflection you can see that this argument is false:
if everyone loves someone, it does not necessarily follow that Joan loves
herself. She might, if the first line is true, love Bill or Pete. *If* we said Joan
was the only person in the world, *then* it would have to follow that she loved
herself, given the first line's truth. Now, although it may seem difficult to
swallow, the kind of logical systems behind the computer could not say,
as you just did, that the argument stated above is false—they would go on
forever and ever checking through sentences and never get the result. I say
this seems hard to swallow, and you just have to take it from me (if you do)
that really the kind of things computers are based on do not and cannot solve
so simple a question. I would have to refer you to some of the literature for
you to understand what I am saying—and that literature is pretty tough.
(If you feel up to making a start you could look at the work of the Oxford
mathematician Roger Penrose or the philosopher Crispin Wright).

But really this just brings home to us what we could realize in other
ways: the symbol crunching of computers does not mean they really understand, as you do in a conscious act of insight, what the symbols *mean*. The
philosopher John Searle brings this out with his story of the "Chinese room."
In the Chinese room there is a man who understands no Chinese. But he has
a graph with Chinese symbols on it. The graph tells him that when he sees a
little token or a group of tokens come through a hatch in front of him, then
he must put such and such a combination of tokens with Chinese characters
on them into an out-hatch behind him. The "combiner" of symbols, the man

inside the little room, does not understand Chinese. But given the program, a Chinese person who came up to the in-slot of the little room and put in symbols saying, for instance, "How are you?" would receive a little set of symbols saying, "Very well thank you," in the out-tray. The point is that the man inside can do the work without understanding, without having a conscious insight into Chinese as could a mechanism, a computer, by which he could be replaced.

If, therefore, there is a level or area specific to us as thinking and choosing human beings, as we see identified in cognitional structure, what might it be to think of that as in some sense nonmaterial?

Reflection on some of the things we have already said about human understanding can help us here. First, understanding, or having an insight, goes beyond mere imagining or picturing. When we imagine or picture something, the images we make do depend totally on our sense experience, on what has come in through our senses. But philosophers in different periods and the drift of modern science both witness that understanding or conceiving goes beyond the mental picturing, which is dependent on the physical, material sense organs. So in modern science one works out mathematical theories that we can understand but cannot literally picture: we can, for instance, work out the maths of the theory of four-dimensional space. But our imagination limps behind because our senses only sense in three dimensions, and our imaginations depend on the senses. This is the point that Quine made to Bryan Magee, as we saw above. Since science talks about entities that we cannot sense, it talks of entities we cannot literally imagine. Descartes knew this, and his example is, perhaps, something we can more readily grasp. He pointed out that we can understand, conceive, and work out the math of a thousand-sided object, but we cannot imagine it. If scientific method has assisted in bringing home a point that philosophers have made in the past, that conceiving goes beyond sense-dependent imagining, then what can we say of the nature of insight, understanding, conception?

As we saw above in our section on form and matter, our insights into the data grasp a "form" or "intelligible pattern" in the data that may or may not be something we could construct an adequate model of in the imagination. Take as an example of an insight grasping a "form," the form that is Euclid's (the ancient Greek father of geometry) definition of a circle. Euclid defined a circle as a series of coplanar points equidistant from the center. You have to imagine a series of dots all equally distant from the center of a circle; if some of the dots are nearer or farther away from the center, you clearly won't have a circle. When the insight, the definition, here grasps the intelligible form of circle, it "abstracts" "or leaves behind" the matter in a sense, as we said above. That is, the insight leaves aside or abstracts from the particularity of the particular drawing in front of it. It reaches an understanding of "circularity" that is not dependent on the circle here and now before it from which it abstracted the idea. One is aware that the definition of "circularity" arrived at can apply to any and all circles, existent or nonexistent. The form I have in my mind is not linked or intrinsically conditioned by any one particular image of a circle.

If someone were to look inside my head when I was thinking of Euclid's definition, perhaps he *would* see imaginative constructs of circles and lines or brain material organized in some way parallel to such images. But that would not be "seeing" or sensing the insight, the act of understanding. For the insight abstracts from this particular image. *It regards circularity in general, circles of all sizes and dimensions—but there can't be any actual, material circles that do not have particular dimensions. So the form grasped in the insight is not that kind of thing. It literally has no material space-time dimensions like the actual circles drawn in the world do. If it did, it would be a particular one of them—but it ain't.*

Perhaps some words of Aquinas will make the point more succinctly than I have above. He writes that our soul is not material, for,

> were it composed of matter and form, the forms of things would be received into it in all their concrete individuality, so that it would know only the singular, as the senses do, which receive forms [images, pictures] of things in a physical organ; for materiality is the principle that individuates form. (*Summa Theologica*, I, q. 75, a. 5)

A final area worth considering philosophically that has to do with our subject is data provided by parapsychology, near-death experiences, and the like. It is interesting to note how many distinguished philosophers have taken this kind of evidence seriously and have been serious students and researchers in the field. One can mention British philosophers such as Henry Sidgwick (d. 1900), H. H. Price (d. 1984), C. D. Broad (d. 1971), and others such as C. J. Ducasse (d. 1969). It is perhaps interesting to note that the antireligious philosopher Anthony Flew takes such data very seriously. He argues that, although some is due to fraud or wishful thinking, there is an enormous amount of data difficult to deny that we should take seriously. It is interesting to see how Flew, a philosopher who would rather dismiss all this kind of evidence, is honest and well-informed enough to take it very seriously, which he does in such books as *The Logic of Mortality* (Oxford: Blackwell, 1987). How then does Flew deal with such apparent evidence for life after death? Well, in the end he simply expresses the hope, the faith, that it will turn out to be evidence we can explain in a materialist way, but he freely admits that on the face of it there is evidence here that runs counter to materialist expectations (see chapter 10 of Flew's book). In a way, then, Flew, just like Quine, is admitting that materialism is a position of faith. Interestingly, another renowned antireligious philosopher of the last century, Bertrand Russell, was even more open than Flew to the evidence for a nonmaterial element to persons coming from parapsychological research. In an essay written in the 1930s Russell admitted that much of the anecdotal evidence for survival after death was impressive and that if this evidence continued to grow we would have to accept the belief in life after death as reasonable (see footnotes to his "Do We Survive Death?" in Russell, *Why I Am not a Christian* [London: Allen and Unwin, 1957]).

*Chapter 6*

# A Short Introduction to Ethics

## Introduction

In this chapter we will attempt to build on the approach that we developed in chapter 2 and extend our reflections into ethics. In the whistle-stop tour of the history of philosophy in chapter 4, we saw how at the very dawn of the philosophical tradition of the West we find the raising of ethical questions: Socrates' persistent questioning of the beliefs and attitudes of his fellow Athenians on moral topics. Socrates had a burning concern with these questions: What should I do? What is right? What is wrong action? How should we live out our lives, as individuals, communities?

We know how in our pluralistic modern West similar ethical questions resound: What is right and wrong in biomedical ethics? What of euthanasia or abortion? At the root of these questions, or the answers to them, are ethical views on the basic goods of human life, on what human beings are, and on what their moral responsibilities should be. We know too that these questions are asked in a culture where the sheer drift toward simple consumerist satisfaction and materialism pervades the media and public life, where very often people feel, if they get as far as thinking of ethics, that the safe and politically correct answer must be, "Well, it's whatever's right for you, isn't it?"

What we shall do in this chapter is present a way of arguing for a basic objective morality, a way that extends the kind of work we have already done on cognitional structure. We will then critically examine some of the more influential ethical views in philosophy and culture. Necessarily this will all be rather brief, for this is a short introduction to this area of philosophy, pointing you in the direction of further reading and work.

## From Knowing to Deciding and Doing

In chapter 2 we counted three levels of cognitional structure: (1) level of experience, (2) level of understanding, and (3) level of judgment. Now we are going to add a fourth level: the level of responsibility, the moral level. Levels 1, 2, and 3 are the levels on which we come to know fact, the real. Level 4 is the level on which we come to know value, the good, the right action, and on which we decide to follow through on that moral knowledge and succeed or fail to do so. On level 1 we said we had to be *attentive* to the data of experience; on level 2 to be *intelligent* in asking questions, having insights, formulating hypotheses, and the like; on level 3 we had to be *reasonable* in assessing our ideas, insights—are they true or probably true of reality? On this fourth level we are to add that we should be *responsible* in trying to understand what the moral implications are concerning the facts we have ascertained through the three levels in coming to know.

We said at the beginning of chapter 2 that we should not be misled by the language of levels. Our thinking and acting occur in a complex flow of consciousness. In that flow we could be thinking about judging an issue while our mind is also wandering onto the level of understanding on another issue, and also we could be admiring the sunset. What is important about talk of "levels," and we can now apply this to the level of responsibility, is that we cannot judge until we have understood on some issue, and we cannot understand unless we have had some experience of some data to ask questions about. Similarly with level 4. We cannot ask questions like "what should I do?" or "what is the right or wrong course of action here?" about nothing. We need to have come across some facts that we then ask moral questions about. So I have now established that those movements in the fog were someone trapped in mud and sinking. What should I do? Well, get them out. It would not be the same situation if the facts had turned out to be that it was a fisherman in waders moving out to cast.

Just as in the case of the other levels in coming to know, we are moved onto this fourth level of responsibility by the raising of a question. So in the three levels of coming to know, one is moved from the level of experience to the level of understanding by the raising of the question "What is that?" And one is moved from the level of intelligence to the level of reasonable judgment by asking the further question "Is it so? Is my hypothesis, insight, idea, hunch true of reality?" Now it is a further question that moves us on to the fourth level of responsibility: "Well, given that the facts are such and such, what should I do about it?" "What is the right course of action?" Of course one can be asking in a very wide-ranging way, "What should I do?" and mean one's whole life or one's whole moral stance. But then that is again asking about something of which one has some knowledge.

Let us take a closer look at some of the conscious activities on this fourth level. First, we can notice that I am *consciously willing* to do things before I ever operate on this fourth level. So, spontaneously I look at a beautiful sunset without stopping to choose in any deliberate way. I also spontaneously fall prey to wonder, as Aristotle pointed out, and enter into asking questions and operating on the levels of coming to know. The fourth level only becomes operative if I stop to make a choice: maybe I should not linger any longer over this sunset; it's time to help get the children into bed; perhaps I must stop thinking over this issue because I have other responsibilities to meet. A second element in the area of our responsible actions, moral actions, are *feelings*. Feelings are vital to us as human beings; they are the stuff and momentum of all our actions. When we come to make a choice, it is feelings, one way or another, that present choices to us as attractive. I would not think about breaking off writing this, unless the feeling of hunger and the attractive prospect of my sandwiches were not to come to mind. But the important thing is that we have a freedom with regard to our feelings. Clearly, this freedom can be diminished by extreme states of psychological pressure: if you are literally shell-shocked you just run for cover. But any of the choices we can be said to be responsible for, even the ones that have very strong emotions or feelings attached to them, pulling us one way or another, are choices that we can determine by the use of our reflective capacities, by the activities of our responsibility. So on the fourth level there is a process involved in choice, rather like the level 3 activities of making a judgment of fact. On level 4 we ask, "What is it right to do? What should I or anyone do in this situation?" So level 4 also involves *moral questions*.

We may deliberate at some length in trying to reach a *moral judgment* about what is right or wrong to do. That deliberation could involve further reflection on the facts, and/or further reflection about the values involved. One might refer to important moral sources, talk to friends, try to find out what the church teaches on this, perhaps even move into philosophical reflection on the ethical issues. But most of our moral judgments are ones that have become habitual. And so we can act with greater or lesser speed in coming to a decision. On the basis of our moral judgments, then, we can move to *decision* about what to do in this particular case.

A further point of comparison and contrast between the judgments we make on level 3 and those made on level 4 is that moral judgments settle what *ought to be* the case, whereas factual judgments (level 3) settle what *is* the case. But a mystery concerning human beings is, as St. Paul says, "For I do not do the good I want, but the evil I do not want is what I do" (Rom 7:19). Human beings can consciously fail to follow through on the decisions they know are good. The Greeks knew this mystery of human failure in the will and called it *Akrasia*. It is conscious inconsistency between what one knows morally and what one does. This the existentialists call inauthenticity and Christians call sin. Another more familiar term for this fourth level of conscious, intentional, responsible activities is conscience.

In the light of these considerations concerning the level of responsibility and the other material we have studied on cognitional structure, we can add here a few remarks about the question of human *freedom*. If we are not free as human beings in our choices, then there is no point in blaming or praising anyone for anything. It would be as pointless as blaming a lion for eating a zebra or a spider for eating a fly: "That's just their nature," we rightly say. The Christian religion indicates that if we were not free, then we could not truly love God, we could not sin, nor would we need redemption.

When we look at this question of freedom, what are we thinking of? We are saying that if I did *x* in my life I was not *necessitated* in doing so; I was not *forced* to do so by something other than myself, outside me, in such a way that I was not responsible for it. Of course there are not only small everyday decisions that we consider here but momentous changes of life: choices of vocation to religious life, priesthood, marriage, religious conversion. Much that we have said already earlier in this book has a bearing on our question, and our brief look at this area can involve drawing to mind again arguments we have already heard and points made earlier.

So we saw in our metaphysics chapter that the modern scientific worldview has moved away from the eighteenth-century vision of the world and all things in it, including for some philosophers the view of human beings as one gigantic clock: a fixed, necessary, determined mechanism that will move along the same lines forever. In a world, rather, of statistical emergence and development there is thought to be a real "freedom" in the way different "ecologies" of the physical, biological, and animal emerge over time. This reflects too on the question of human freedom: it in some way continues what is there elsewhere in nature. This, however, is where we must make an important distinction. For we may say that a subatomic particle is "free" in moving this way or that, but we mean something more specific with human freedom. For human freedom has to do with being attentive, intelligent, reasonable, and responsible, that is, acting on the four levels. Here our previous discussions of reductionism come in. Those who deny human freedom are denying that we are free to consider responsibly a proposal and to go this way or that. But really what they are doing is saying that we are necessitated or controlled by something outside our own conscious intelligence, reasonableness, responsibility.

We are back then with the kind of view we saw with the behaviorist psychologist in the last chapter. His view is that we think this way or that, decide this way or that, because we are forced, necessitated, in doing so by some subrational force (e.g., the psychological aversions inbuilt through early childhood formation). But we saw that all such views are self-destructive. For they say we never really think or do anything for good reason but would have us agree with their views because they are put forward for sufficient reason. Let us put this another way. When anyone argues that I should take such and such a view, perhaps a view of human knowing or of morality, they are saying that I ought to choose their view: that I ought to be attentive, intelligent, reasonable, and responsible in thinking it through and accepting it. But then this *ought* is an appeal to me to choose to be attentive, intelligent, etc. Otherwise what is being said is that I will just have to accept or have to reject this view, not depending on the free exercise of my rational powers but on some nonrational force (my potty training, fear of treading on lines in the pavement, or other phobias).

Further, our freedom is attested to, sadly, by the mystery of human weakness and sin. That the good that I see I should do does not necessitate my doing it is shown by the way, in sin, I can fail to carry through on a good choice. Although sin witnesses to our freedom, it is not an indication of a growth in freedom but rather the opposite. For the more I sin, the more I become a slave to forces that curtail my freedom.

## Arguing for a Basic View of Morality or Ethics

The kind of argument that turns other arguments back on themselves to show self-destructive elements in them was used by us in our chapter on epistemology. You can see from the discussion of the behaviorist view that we have just given that this kind of argument can be extended into ethics or the theory of morality. In this section we will use such arguments in order to ground a basic view of morality. This basic view will be rather generally presented in such a chapter as this.

What is the good, or what are the goods, that human beings should pursue in life? Some will answer that they know the answer to this question from their religious faith, but how could we get nearer to an answer on the basis of human reason alone? Attempting to do so is very important from the perspective of the Catholic faith. For the Catholic position is that there is a "natural law" that is, as St Paul suggests in Romans 2, "written on their hearts, to which their own conscience also bears witness" (2:15)—Jews and Greeks, Christians and pagans alike. This Catholic position in morality is vitally important in our modern pluralist world. The Catholic Church does not criticize non-Catholic citizens who do not go to Mass on Sunday; that depends on the gift of faith. But she does reason and work against abortion, euthanasia, and unjust and oppressive political and economic systems around the world, presenting reasons accessible to all for doing so.

Different ethical philosophies, ones that we can see operative in our culture (not simply left in the ivory tower of a university), hold that differing things are the goods or values that human beings should choose, on the basis of which society should be organized, on the basis of which actions should be judged as wrong or right. So *hedonism* claims that the only good in life is pleasure. *Emotivism* says that right or wrong, good or bad, are things that we decide simply on the basis of feelings; our moral judgments are not reasonable but are like expressions of taste—you like Gustav Mahler, and I do not; I like bitter beer while you prefer lager. This is a form of *moral relativism*. It is widespread in the West. The view runs, "Whatever is right for you is right for you." Each individual can make up his or her own morality—no one should interfere with him or her. *Marxists* have a kind of morality that is akin to that of the *utilitarians*. The maxim is "the greatest good for the greater number," and one holds that "the ends justify the means." So in order to get the perfect Marxist state one can do anything on the way justified by one's goal. St. Paul's maxim that "I should not do evil so that good may come" is rejected. Various forms of this kind of moral thinking have been further developed in the twentieth century by *consequentialists* or *proportionalists*. For them a good act is that which maximizes good effects. There are, then, no absolute moral norms. What you can do is add up the tally and do literally anything if you think it will have the best outcome in the long run. The older versions of this view, of philosophers like Jeremy Bentham and John Stuart Mill in the nineteenth century, linked it to hedonism: you had to maximize pleasure units. But the twentieth-century proportionalist also allows other goods than pleasure: the key thing is that there are no absolutes; you can do anything with the best consequences. We should also mention here Nietzschean morality. The German philosopher Friedrich Nietzsche rejected what he saw as mealy mouthed nineteenth-century middle-class Christian morality and proposed an idea of morality as a kind of personal endeavor like a work of art. There are no societal rules; the main thing is risk and dare and novel doing. This is "beyond good and evil," as he put it. This is the kind of view that fed into some of the "glory of war and chaos" cults among Fascists and Nazis after the First World War. Finally in our list we can mention the complete *moral skeptic*: he holds that we do not know what is right or wrong, good or bad.

Largely opposed to what these theories have to say are theories such as those of Aristotle, Plato, Aquinas, Kant, and many others in the Western tradition. Such views, although at variance among themselves on many issues, would hold that one can reach an objective view of morality on the basis of which one could say that certain acts were wrong, certain right, and that one could know that certain kinds of acts were good or bad, irrespective of circumstances, that is, irrespective of the consequences of these acts stretching into the future.

Another point we can look at here is one made by our friend David Hume. Hume pointed out that many writers whose works he had read went on and on about how things are in nature, how human beings behave, about how God is, and so forth, and then suddenly leapt to this conclusion: therefore human beings *ought* to do such and such. Hume's point was, then, that one cannot get an *ought* from an *is*. That is, because one says that such a thing is in such and such a way, this does not entail that it *ought* to be like this. Hume's argument appears skeptical and destructive of any natural law view. But as we shall argue below, it is not destructive of the natural law position of Aquinas and Aristotle when that is properly understood. It is, however, destructive of many arguments "from nature," and indeed Hume is a great ally here. For his objection is like acid poured on the froth of many silly ideologies of what human beings should be like. So in the last two centuries one sees social Darwinists of one kind or another arguing that since in "nature" the law is the "survival of the fittest," so in the human world that ought to be our morality. Another version of this is found in the views of people who go on about our genes being "selfish," the implication being, presumably, that since we are made up of "selfish genes," it is only our nature to be selfish. The nonsense in such views is evident when one considers that they have begun by projecting anthropomorphic, or human, qualities onto nonhuman beings to start with and then end up by trying to draw lessons for human morality from the behavior of nonhuman entities. Other views like this say that morality is to be seen in terms of "survival of the species." However well intentioned such arguments are, they fall outside of Hume's logical point. For human beings can and do ask questions, which other species do not and cannot ask, such as "Why perpetuate the species? Is it all a big waste of time?" One cannot draw an *ought* from an *is* in this way.

How, then, to argue for a basic view of morality, a view akin to that of Aristotle and Aquinas on natural law, in the context of all these rival theories? Well, let us first imagine all the various contenders stuck in a seminar room somewhere, arguing for the positions they hold. Then let us notice something very important about all the contenders in this philosophical debate. Implicit in all their arguing is the view that *(a) one ought to get to know the truth about morality and (b) form one's action accordingly*. In other words they are all, in doing what they are doing, showing a common commitment to being attentive, intelligent, reasonable, and responsible. Insofar as they are arguing, they are trying to establish their positions in this way. So in arguing for a common, basic view, what one can do is make this *implicit* commitment to these values *explicit* and recognize them as such.

Let us look at what we mean here in more detail. Let us take the moral skeptic, for example. He is arguing that none of the other views of morality hold water. But in that case what is he saying? He is saying that if one is to be authentic, one ought to be attentive, intelligent, and reasonable as he is doing and come up with the correct view that none of the other views are compelling. He is not, for example, just being silly or stupid or frivolous. Therefore truth is a *basic good, a value* for him. He is saying that people with other views—Christians, Marxists maybe—*should not* tell other people to accept these views and act on them. He is saying we *ought not* to accept a moral view as true and we *ought not* to act on the basis of that moral view if that moral view is false. He is showing that his own nature is a dynamic commitment to moral truth and consistent action with that truth. If one is arguing that one does not have to get at moral truth in order to do the good, one is committed to the truth of that; one is saying you *ought* to agree with me because what I am saying is true. We are back, then, with the kind of marmalade-stutterer arguments of chapter 2. Anyone who argues against the view that one should get at the moral truth and act accordingly is saying that one should get at the moral truth and act accordingly.

There are two moral absolutes here: (a) that one gets to the moral truth and (b) that one acts accordingly. Absolute (b) is just our conscious awareness that to hold $x$ as what is morally required of us and then to do not-$x$ is what we mean by inauthenticity, moral evil, or sin. It is the basic consciousness of inconsistent behavior, of sin. It is something as basic in us as our awareness of the law of noncontradiction. What of some of our other contenders mentioned above? What of Hume, for example? Well, it is true that one cannot "get" an ought from an is in the way Hume describes it. There is, however, a way of getting an "ought" from an "is." And it is a way that, we can notice, everyone involved in the debate is committed to, Hume included. So when Hume argues that we cannot get an ought from an is, he is implicitly committed to the view that one *ought not* to say that one can get an ought from an is, and one *ought not* to go around preaching to people on the basis of one's faulty deductions from nature (the laws of the jungle) telling them what to do. Thus, like anyone else, Hume is committed in practice to the basic implicit view we have outlined: *one ought to get to know the moral truth and act accordingly.*

What of the hedonist? Well, does he settle for the view that gives a lovely tingle in his leg? In other words, does he accept as true, as *good to accept*, the view that gives most pleasure? If he does, then he disqualifies himself from discussion among those who want, through the exercise of their intelligence and reason, to get to know the moral truth. The moral truth could be totally uncomfortable, totally devoid of pleasure; we do not know in advance if it will be pleasurable. All we know in advance is that we ought to get to know the truth and act accordingly, and if pleasure waylays us from that then it is not a value.

What of the proportionalist? This is perhaps a little more tricky to grasp. There are many current criticisms of proportionalism. Some point to the fact that proportionalism, adding up future consequences to decide here and now what is wrong and right, destroys all individual rights. Given particular circumstances where you think it would benefit greater numbers in the future you could, for example, endlessly torture the innocent. According to proportionalism, maybe Hitler and Stalin will turn out to be great moral heroes when, down through the centuries, it is realized that the consequences of their acts of torture and destruction in the twentieth century had consequences that somehow led to many people being happy in years to come; after all, lots of technical life-improving inventions come out of modern warfare.

Besides considering such objections to proportionalism, we can note here that our self-destructive argument can also cut off proportionalism at the root. For proportionalism says that no act is always wrong or always right; you have to add up the consequences. But the point we can make from our observations above is this: in arguing as he does, the proportionalist is committed, as are all the others, to the view that one ought to get to know the correct moral theory and act accordingly. And we can add: *irrespective of the consequences*. That is, the proportionalist must be committed to intelligence, reasonableness, and responsibility in establishing his theory. He cannot say that the true moral theory should be adopted in terms of how many good consequences follow from adopting it. That would be to beg the question as to whether his theory was already known to be correct or not. No, we have seen that to argue against the position that what one must do is accept the true moral theory and act accordingly is to show that one implicitly accepts it. Thus one can establish the view on morality in this way. But if one has, one has established it without any reference to what the future may hold, what the consequences of one accepting this theory may be. In a deep sense the consequences are *irrelevant* to the issue. Simply here and now I know that I must accept a true moral theory as true and base my actions on it. Acknowledging these demands is acknowledging something basic, absolute about myself.

If truth and doing the good are basic goods, then, and if absolute moral norms can be based on them, are there other such basic goods? Well, if we think of our philosophers in the seminar debate, we can realize that if they implicitly accept these goods, other basic goods, values, are connected immediately with them. For instance, they could not be arguing without the goods or values of life and sufficient health—they could not be going for very long without food. Nor would they be there in the seminar room if two people, a community, had not joined together to give them life—their parents. Further, to think or argue coherently without pathological disturbance is to have had some kind of half-decent upbringing, education, where other human beings, our parents but others also, have helped us, have been our friends—thus Aristotle's emphasis on the fundamental value that is friendship. So to will to know the truth and do it is also, in the world in which we exist, to will, implicitly at least, that many other things be in place.

This is, however, only the lightest sketch of all that is entailed in thinking out an ethical theory along these lines. But you can see that the moral absolutes of (a) "come to know the truth" and (b) "act accordingly" bring with them further values or basic goods on which they depend. When we spell out such further basic goods we will see that we have arrived at a natural law position on morality in line with that of Aristotle and St. Thomas Aquinas.

## The Good and Reality: The Communal Good

We can argue for the following:

being = intelligible and reasonable;
good = intelligible and reasonable;
therefore, good = being.

How is this so? When we say an action of a human being is evil, we tend to say things like, "it was totally unreasonable," "absurd," "did not make sense." If we can understand why someone did something, really explain it, then we do not say that it was absurd or unreasonable in this way. If someone hurts someone, and the assailant was really mentally deranged, we do not blame them and say what they did was irresponsible. To attribute irresponsibility to someone we suppose that they had some degree of freedom with regard to their actions. A sin, an evil action, by an agent that does what they know they should not do is, quite literally, an absurdity, an unintelligibility. If we could give reasons it would not be absurd or unintelligible; it would not be wrong.

For St. Thomas Aquinas evil is a privation, a *privatio boni*, a lack of being or reality; it is the absence of the reality or being that should have come to pass, that morally *ought* to have been, but through human sin did not come to be so. Let us consider an example. We are at a birthday party. I have had my fair share of cakes, but now I act greedily. I take the extra cake that was Uncle Fred's, left for him so that he could have it when he gets in from work. Now the "realities" involved are not evil. The physiology of my arm movements as I reach out to take the cake is good, my arms are in working order, just as they should be, just so my digestive system and the delicious taste of the cake: this is all really so, and is all good. What is evil is that what should have happened did not. To be just and fair I should have left the cake, but I did not. The evil is not, then, all the realities, beings, involved in the situation; these are all good. It is rather the absence: the absence of the situation that should have been realized, given the knowledge of right and wrong here on my part.

What then of satan? According to Scripture and the dogmatic teaching of the Catholic faith, satan and evil spirits exist (e.g., see Creed of Council Lateran IV). Are these not actually evil entities? Insofar as anything exists it is good, created by God, this is also Catholic faith. With regard to satan and evil spirits we have to say that given the immense potential for good that these great intelligent beings were created for, it is precisely their failure, their refusal to be as they should, that is the immense lack and absence, privation, in their case.

Turning briefly, and finally, to the good as communal, we can note the way that political and social life needs to be understood as functioning for the flourishing of human persons in community. And these ways of organization, if they are to be good, just, and fair, must be based on an objective morality rooted in a vision of what human persons are about, what their rights and duties as persons are. We saw how we could begin to argue for such an objective morality, a natural law, starting with the moral absolutes that human beings should come to know the moral truth and act accordingly, consistently, and that human beings are always also involved in community, in the community of family, friends, and so forth. If in society we do not have some kind of objective vision like this, we are not fostering a wonderful free democracy where everyone can choose a morality that is simply okay for them. Rather, we risk the destruction of any kind of social pluralism that is based on the dignity of the person in community. This is the theme of the closing sections of Pope John Paul II's encyclical *Veritatis Splendor*.

To see the danger here we can reflect on the implications for society and the political process of an out-and-out relativism in morals or an extreme libertarianism. We often hear the idea around today that what is permissible in society is "whatever is right for you," and then, perhaps if the person is pressed to think this through a little they add, "as long as that does not interfere with what other people want to do." First, we can note that if someone does add the second statement to the first they have, in fact, moved beyond a mere relativism. They are actually saying that "you should not do $x$ if $x$ interferes with another's wishes, desires." But the view that society's purpose is for the fulfillment of as many wishes as possible of its members is often not thought through consistently. This kind of view, known as libertarianism, was proposed by thinkers such as Mill in the last century. It is opposed to a paternalism in society, which implies that society takes the role of a parent in directing peoples' lives. Mill, and libertarians, say, "Fine, paternalism is right for the parental relationship to children. We do make children do things for their own good, which they do not want to do, but after we grow up, all this must change—then maximal freedom is the social goal." Interestingly, Mill made an exception, a very significant exception when one thinks about it, to the freedoms the state should allow: he denied that the state should allow its citizens to sell themselves into slavery. In other words, one could have laws preventing this. Why, if that is what an adult wants to do? Well, Mill replies, the state is there to maximize freedom, but selling oneself into slavery is a destruction of that very freedom itself that the state is there to foster; it is a kind of suicide. There is much in this point made by Mill, a point that he did not develop very far. And it leads us on to think about the un-thought-out nature of the idea that society should let people do whatever they like as long as they don't get in other people's way.

The problem with this view, when one thinks about it, is that it does *not think through what is fair or unfair, just or unjust interference*. If I send you promotional literature following trade laws, in doing so, you may really hate the way I am interfering in your breakfast peace, but is that permissible interference or not? The rub is that ultimately one must come back to a reflection on the basic goods of human persons, on what they are called to be, and so forth if one is to have a hope of consistently thinking through the business of fair and just or unfair and unjust interference in the activities of others. What can happen otherwise is the development of a state of affairs where society does not even attempt to justify its actions, where, in effect, it just becomes a big bully or a big terrorist. So on what grounds does society pursue, prosecute, and imprison a certain group of terrorists? If it has a morality of "whatever's right for you," it is acting totally inconsistently in doing this to the terrorists—it is just a form of terrorism itself. No, it needs a rationale for deciding that these forms of violent actions by the terrorist group are immoral and nonpermissible forms of interference in the lives of other citizens. And ultimately, if consistent, this rationale will have to be a full-blown account of the goods of persons in community, including a view of the rights and duties of persons based on these goods, which rules out some forms of interference as immoral.

*Chapter 7*

# Philosophy of Religion and the Question of God

## Reasoning to God's Existence

The arguments for the existence of God are all ways of thinking through an answer to ultimate questions like these: Why is there anything rather than nothing? What's the meaning of it all? Is there any purpose to my life ultimately? Is there an ultimate ground for the goodness we see in the world? God, then, is the ultimate answer to humankind's question for meaning and value in life.

Fundamentally this type of argument indicates that for there to be an explanation, an intelligible account of the world, there must be sufficient reason for it. Those in the Humean tradition, like John Stuart Mill, who respond by saying, "But then who made God?" miss the point. The positing of God as the fundamental explanation is precisely the positing of that which explains, provides sufficient reason both for "itself" (himself) and for all the contingent beings (nonnecessary, non-self-explanatory beings) that make up the world. To suggest that the "world" could just as well do this is to miss the point, since by the "world" we mean precisely the totality of contingent beings, and interrelations of beings, that require explanation, that are contingent.

Similarly to posit infinite regress is to change the subject without meeting the issue. The insights behind infinite regress can be expressed equally well by positing some mutual causing sequence: say *A* causes *B*, *B* causes *C*, *C*

causes *A*; we can even think of this as forever happening and even occurring as a set of simultaneous causes. But again, it does not meet the issue,
as there is no explanation for the existence of any of the causal agents nor
for the whole setup. Such regress is not, then, "inconceivable" in a certain
sense but is unintelligible; that is, it does not suffice as an adequate explanation of what exists.

When we say God is "inconceivable" we should mean that we do understand something about God, but we do not have direct insight into a being
that exists necessarily: who, if we were to understand his nature, we would
also know exists. But without such a being nothing else would exist, and
we know that that is not the case: I exist, things exist.

Fundamentally the various "ways" as found in the thought of St. Thomas
Aquinas or arguments for God are all arguments that point to the fact that
reality is intelligible; therefore there is a sufficient explanation for reality.
At the heart of these arguments, then, is a *principle of intelligibility*. We can
then go on to identify the various external causes of a being—the efficient,
exemplary, and final causes, which we saw in the chapter on metaphysics, as
various types of intelligible explanation of why something exists. Arguments
from design in the universe, from the intelligible ordering in the world, are
also ultimately about asking, "Why do these developmental structures with
their intelligible forms exist as they do?"

One can point out that to deny the *principle of intelligibility*, stating *that
what is, is the intelligible* is also self-refuting. It is to claim to know that
reality is not that which is known by intelligence and reason and thus defined
in some broad sense by the requirements of intelligence, while at the same
time employing intelligence and reason in claiming to know what is really
the case—about, say, the powers and limitations of human knowledge itself
or some other reality.

Either we know nothing or we know something. If we know something
then that is a "knowable": it is isomorphic or cognate with our knowing.
And our knowing is acquired through intelligence and reasonable judgment,
so the known is the intelligible and reasonable. If we deny that we know
anything or deny that reality, being, is the intelligible, we enter a contradiction because we are really claiming to know something and are therefore
claiming that what we know is the knowable or intelligible.

The principle of intelligibility is, then, akin to the principle of noncontradiction. The principle of noncontradiction states that something cannot
both be the case and not be the case at the same time. It cannot be true that
*both A and not-A* are true. To deny this is to operate with it. For to deny the

principle is to make a claim to truth that rules out as false the denial of that claim (the claim being about the principle of noncontradiction itself).

Now when we know noncontradiction it is not because this particular instance of reality we are thinking about comes with a label saying "noncontradiction applies here." No, rather, we judge individual instances in the light of noncontradiction because we are aware it applies generally and the particular case is to be judged in the light of it; so too with the principle of intelligibility. So too, therefore, with causality of various types, which are aspects of that broader concept of the intelligibility of being.

We need to grasp, then, that talk of *causation* is precisely an unpacking of aspects of the intelligibility required to explain why what is the case is so.

Let us recall the different types of external cause that need to be invoked to explain the existence of a contingent being, such as a bridge. Let us also recall that sufficient explanation does not come from one type of cause alone but from all the causes together.

We identified, in the chapter on metaphysics, the efficient cause, the final cause, and the exemplary cause. The efficient cause was illustrated by the effort and labor to get the stones of the bridge in place, but the "why this?" question is not answered by that cause alone but by that cause in conjunction with the final and exemplary causes. The exemplary cause means the blueprint, the *intelligent plan* in accord with which the bridge is constructed, and intimately connected with this cause is the final cause: without the end in view, without the *goal as intended*, the thing would not come about.

We can note at once that both the exemplary cause and the final cause involve understanding and knowledge. Understanding is intrinsic to them. Without understanding, without knowing capacities, one cannot conceive of a design nor can one conceive of an end, a goal. Thus in order for God to be the explanation of contingent reality it must be that God is a knowing being, for without knowing God cannot be the required exemplary cause nor the required final cause of what is in the real world.

As we have argued, we "knowers" can know ourselves to be beings who consciously understand and reason. But we know ourselves as at once contingent: I might not be. Nothing in the idea, nature, or intelligible form of "knower" as understood means that one has to exist, or must exist. By raising and answering the question "Am I a knower? Does a knower exist?" I can come to know that, as a matter of fact, one does exist: I exist. Anything else one encounters in the world is in the same boat, whether this is in science or in any other cognitive enterprise. We only ever encounter beings whose essence, their "what," is such that just by thinking it we do not thereby know that it must exist. Everything we encounter or know (as best we can) is contingent, not necessary.

If contingent things are nonnecessary then they do not arise with necessity, otherwise they would be God, "part of God," but, on the contrary, they are contingent by nature. But we say that the principle of intelligibility (which we cannot deny without contradiction) means that God must provide sufficient reason, explanation, for what is. If what comes forth from the necessary being, God, is, therefore, not itself necessary and not merely arbitrary (for the arbitrary lacks sufficient explanation—it remains unintelligible), then it comes forth in a way that is like our free acts: free acts cause things, give an intelligible explanation of why there is this or that, but do so as nonnecessary. It is not necessary that I take the dog out for her last night visit into the garden at 9:30 p.m. rather than 10:00 p.m., but the fact that this occurs when it does is a result of my free choice to do it now rather than later, for some intended aim—maybe I want to listen to the 10:00 news. Both the aim in view, of taking her out now so as to . . . , and the plan of doing so (opening the door, calling her) are explained only because I have understanding, knowledge, and also because I will to bring these things about.

Thus, we attribute to God free will akin to our own free will. Without knowledge or will God would not provide sufficient explanation of what is. Because we have reason to affirm that God has something akin to our knowing and willing capacities, we can truly call God "personal."

## Is Opting for Religion a Good Choice?

Those who, like Richard Dawkins, attack religion today claim that religion is not, in fact, a good option. They claim that if one looks at the history of religions and the lives of religious people one sees that religious conviction causes hatred, bigotry, and pride and that religion is thus the cause of many of the evils in the world. Before Dawkins and his allies, philosophers like Bertrand Russell said similar things, and the German philosopher Friederich Nietzsche attacked Christianity in this way too. Nietzsche is often named one of the great "masters of suspicion" along with Karl Marx and Sigmund Freud. These masters of suspicion were out to show that religions such as Christianity in reality curtailed and repressed the true, free, and joyous nature of human beings in the name of myths.

For such thinkers, then, the question "Which religion?" should be met by the answer "None." For them religion is a bad and not a good thing. A first question that arises is whether there is anything that might lead one to object to these objections from a philosophical standpoint. A second question we shall look at here is whether or not, if religion is a good option after all, philosophy might have resources to help us think about whether or not Christianity is the religion to opt for.

## Religion: A Good or an Evil?

Here we cannot go into a detailed analysis of the thought of such representative antireligious thinkers as Russell, Nietzsche, Freud, and Marx, and so our philosophical considerations will be of a more general nature that applies to the kind of objections to religion that their views typify. One can begin by saying that, of course, if one were to sit these different thinkers down together for a conversation of any length one would find that pretty soon quite divergent and violent disagreements would become evident between them on all manner of philosophical issues, including, one would expect, on precisely how and why organized religion was to be critiqued. Further, if we were to proceed to a more detailed analysis of the actual views of these thinkers we would soon find that some of them espoused problematic views on epistemology, metaphysics, and ethics, views that we have in fact critiqued in one way or another in earlier sections of this book, and that these views naturally fed into and influenced philosophical positions they held on religion. Others in the group, like Freud and Marx, had little time for the key areas in philosophy we have discussed and their views on these matters (key for a philosophy of religion) would be found, upon examination, to be naive and uninformed.

We can briefly observe here that while Freud tried to explain away religion as "really" being the expression of a psychological inadequacy and Marx thought that in reality the history of religion was the manifestation of underlying economic forces that controlled it, other thinkers have turned their objections on their heads. Thus, not long after Marx, the great German sociologist and student of history Max Weber (d. 1920) argued that the historical data show quite the reverse of what Marx said: very often we see religious/cultural forces influencing economic styles and trends. As for Freud, early on there was, of course, the alternative of Carl G. Jung's (d. 1961) psychology, which saw religion as a necessary element in human psychological development. More recently the psychologist Paul Vitz, a convert from atheism to Catholicism, has produced a book (*Faith of the Fatherless: The Psychology of Atheism*) in which he examines the lives of several atheistic thinkers like Freud and argues that their atheism was a psychological manifestation of the inadequate relationships they had with their fathers when young. This kind of flipping antireligious arguments on their heads was the hallmark of the apologetics of that renowned Christian "deconstructionist" G. K. Chesterton.

The key objection that seems to arise from the kind of antireligious traditions these thinkers represent is that religion is a *bad* thing, not a good thing, and that we can see this when we look at the lives of individual Christians, say, and at the history of religious rivalry and hatred.

A first response of a Christian philosopher would be one that fully and frankly acknowledges that there is plenty of data to show that such objections to a religion like Christianity have a valid foundation. Very able apologists for Christianity such as G. K. Chesterton and C. S. Lewis (d. 1963) always approached the matter in this candid and honest way. Nevertheless, one also has to say that each historical case has to be carefully examined in the light of up-to-date, unbiased historical scholarship. Justice and fairness are as little served by rehashing massively out-of-date "black legends" from the eighteenth century when we are discussing the Crusades, the history of the Inquisition, and the history of the church and science as they are by denying or offering some tendentious explaining away of the immoral lives of some Renaissance popes.

The importance of such scholarly accounts cannot be underestimated. In a good number of cases they show that the "black legends" have distorted the truth about what Christians or the church did. In other cases they can also help us see just how bad things were. The study of history, however, pursued in an academic fashion, also helps us understand the historically conditioned nature of human perspectives and viewpoints, including our own. Such a historical sense should help us to sympathize to some extent with persons and groups in different periods from our own, even if we can see that they may have accepted or endorsed views that we must say, now, are objectively unethical or less than acceptable. With such a viewpoint in place we can, perhaps, better appreciate in a realistic way the moral progress that Christianity brought about: for instance the way Christianity ended the barbarities of the Roman world seen in the games, or the way over time it destroyed the ancient edifice of slavery. The other side of the coin is that Christianity itself is all about acknowledging human moral weakness and sinfulness.

The last point makes us ask the severe moral critics of Christianity whence will come their strength and hope in time of moral trial. If Christianity has a story full of sinners, it also has a story of incredible moral heroes who are saints, and the reading of good, sound, and scholarly accounts of the lives of saints and holy people is a very important aspect of making a reasoned case for religion, and Christianity in particular. The existential appeal of holy, integrated people for the truth of a religion is indeed great, for if we are looking for a place where God appears to be dynamically operative, then surely we will see it in those who appear to be on the way to full human integration—in those whose lives manifest an integrity and integration between moral truth, human feeling, love of others, and fundamental joy in existence. Further, these persons attribute such growth not to themselves but to the religious tradition in which they are formed and to its spiritual and sacramental resources. While we who read their lives may feel a long way off, we can also feel strengthened by the thought that we can follow the same road and maybe by following it, notice that we are making some slight progress—even if this is only at times not going too far backwards.

Now, there is no question that there are humanists and atheists who have shown heroic courage. But the evidence of a post-Christian society in the West rather tends to confirm that in general, once Christianity is on the wane, then so is the kind of self-giving that goes beyond hedonistic self-satisfaction. And is this not completely understandable? If life is about "eat, drink, for tomorrow we die," then where are we to find the moral courage, the inspiration, and ultimately the love that will take us beyond ourselves to self-sacrifice? If we look at even the noblest of pagan moral philosophies prior to Christianity, perhaps those shown in Stoicism (which partly was contemporaneous with the emergence of the Christian faith), then the greatest vision of the moral human life that the Stoics can present to us, inspiring though it may be, is very poor when compared to the image of what a human person can be, shown in figures such as Mother Teresa of Calcutta, St. Maximilian Kolbe, St. Francis of Assisi, St. Pio of Pietrelcina, or St. Thérèse of Lisieux. Ultimately these people in history show to us that the high demands of human morality are not lived up to, on a day-to-day basis, from a mere human decision but because morality, ethics, is integrated into lives of interpersonal love, a love with a personal God who they believe is incarnate in Jesus of Nazareth.

I come now to the most fundamental issue to do with whether it is a good thing to opt for a religion such as Christianity, and naturally this is connected to all that I have been saying up to this point. I know of no instance, certainly no instance that is in any way convincing, in which a humanist or antireligious thinker has shown that if the universe is meaningless, if all religions are false and the hope of life after death as a fulfillment is illusory, that is *better* than any of these religious beliefs being true. The whole effort of antireligious thought in the last two centuries has been concerned with trying to show that such views of reality are illusory and, perhaps, that Christianity and its history is a force not for good but for evil. But all this has been done pretty much with the presumption that people will perhaps be massively disappointed by the great vision of faith being false, and one has to help them "cheer up" or perhaps just "grow up" and face the stark reality. No one has really tried in any convincing manner to show that the alternative reality is not "stark"; rather, they try to encourage people to face the darkness and simply to find joy where they can. All this seems to point to a general recognition implicit at least in what these critiques say: that it would, naturally, be better if the universe had a purpose, if a good and loving God existed, who would comfort and reward the many millions who die in poverty and under oppression, but that we just have to get used to it that this is not so. Then there can be the regular experiences of failure, boredom, depression, and anxiety when the self-made ideals of an optimistic atheism about human goodness and moral striving seem so terribly shabby and not the kind of "great vision" that help one live as a good person. Compared to the deep-seated interpersonal love of which Christians speak and witness to as helping them through such times and even allowing them to see such times as good, as a source of "grace," the humanist proposals for a power and a moral energy that ground human personal and ethical growth seem poor indeed.

In this way most agnostics, atheists, and humanists point to the *great good* that religion is or would be if it could be lived in a pure form. They do so by the way they imply, in more or less explicit ways, that we just have to be content with something *much less* wonderful, beautiful, and loveable than a Christian vision of the world would propose (since it is not true), and by the way any alternative "optimistic" moral vision they propose comes across as existentially thin and ultimately unsatisfying.

## Is Opting for Religion a Reasonable Choice?

Given that this kind of religious viewpoint is a "great good," then can one be justified in opting for it? Simply because something is a great good one may not be justified, rationally, in choosing it. That the poor of the world could be fed on sand would be a great thing to believe were it true, but we have absolutely no reason to think it so. As we have argued already, however, there is a good deal of evidence and, I would argue, sufficient evidence for a probable judgment that Christianity is true and also that, given this evidence, it is a very good choice to opt for it. We have seen important elements of this evidence already when, earlier in the chapter, we built on the epistemological and metaphysical positions of this book to extend the argument to saying that reason provides foundations for affirming the existence of a personal God (that is, a God who as ultimate explanation also has knowledge and will). We will go on to consider below other elements of interlocking evidence, which, taken together with the arguments for God's existence, provide evidence that is both further evidence for the existence of a personal God and also for the actions and self-revelation of that God in human lives and history. Before we do that, we can consider how this interlocking evidence fits together with the morally good choice of believing and how its interlocking nature is to be characterized.

So we have been arguing above that the choice for the Christian religion is a very good one, given the evidence there is for the effect it has on human lives for overcoming evil and bias, and opening us up to meaning and self-sacrificing actions through an interpersonal love of God. But, while this vision is enormously appealing, if rightly understood, we still need evidence that it is so in order to choose it.

The interconnection between the evidence of its being true and the option of the moral decision to embrace it can be brought out in this way: imagine a rescue team searching frantically to save victims from under the rubble of an earthquake. These expert workers put themselves at great risk in going into fallen buildings to find survivors, and they need to make reasoned estimates, taking into consideration degrees of risk and use of resources (including time and manpower) when they are assessing whether to try this option or that, which may offer chances of finding survivors under the earthquake rubble. Now, suppose under a great pile of such rubble they hear noises. The expert team has to come to a reasoned and good decision whether or not to try to dig there and risk rescuers on the basis of the evidence of the noises they can detect. Is it worth it? What are the chances of that noise being a human person under there, rather than some water or a noise of some machine or even an animal? Perhaps they decide to risk it. They dig and send rescuers down into the perilous situation. Why? Because of the great good of rescuing a human being *and* because there is enough evidence to make the risk worth it.

Similarly, in opting for the good of the Christian religion, we need to take into account both the evidence for its truth and the great good on offer in the choice of it. But, in fact, the great good of doing so is, at once, an important part of the evidence for the truth of Christianity, if we take this in conjunction with our arguments for the existence of a personal God. For if a personal God deliberately created beings that innately seek an ultimate reason for their existence and for a love that takes them beyond self-seeking to objective good, then what was said above about the good of Christian existence is evidence that God is to be found in this religion as willing it. For the desire for fulfillment that one finds written into one's being and thus caused by the ultimate cause of one's being is satisfied in this religion.

The importance of interlocking reasons for belief in religion can be considered in the light of what we have said about reasonable, probable judgments earlier in the book. Most of our judgments in life are probable judgments, being more or less probable. This is so in daily life and in scholarship and science: yes, in science too, as we have seen when we looked at scientific method as a particular instance of our cognitional activity. The progress of science is also marked by the interlocking of various probable pieces of evidence with moral decisions: given the evidence for this line of thought or this or that theory (which is itself made up of multiple smaller theories and pieces of probable evidence), a scientist or a group of scientists decide to spend time, money, and resources pursuing this avenue of investigation rather than that. Science and the courtroom, then, like the religious decision, bring into consideration multiple pieces of evidence that will, perhaps, build into a strong, probable case, which will then ground a moral choice to do this or that as the most reasonable and good thing to do in the circumstances.

Arguing for God's existence and the reasonableness of opting for a religion like Christianity is a matter of looking at cumulative and converging arguments. If a personal God exists, might we not expect God to give us a self-revelation if we have been made as creatures that look for ultimate answers and for goodness and beauty? Arguments for the existence and nature of God support the reasonableness of the idea of a revelation of God, and the evidence for God's self-revelation also supports the reasoned belief in God's existence. This is not a vicious circle or begging the question. As was said above, we often take it in life and take it to be reasonable in a scholarly or scientific arguments to bring in evidence and arguments that give mutual support to one another.

## Miracles

We will now say something about philosophical discussions of miracles, and below we will go on to look at evidence for God's existence and self-revelation from religious experience. But we need to keep in mind as we go along the idea of elements interlocking in the way we have described. Thus, in the case of those very integrated people who we call "saints" we see events and experiences that are claimed to be miraculous. But we should also see that these occurrences (a) fit into lives that themselves appear somewhat "miraculous" as they are lives of goodness and love that, from the perspective of human history, seem to be out of the normal; (b) further, the people in question witness to the fact that what they achieve in heroism comes not from their own power but from God; and (c) the lives of such people, which include particular "miraculous" events, express and witness to, are evidence of, an interpersonal dialogue with God. And, we should at once add, as we have noted above, the lives of such people (if we study them through properly and soberly conducted works of biography) are not "cut off" from the rest of us, since we also can glimpse in our daily lives similar experiences, maybe on occasion dramatic ones, in which we can, by following their lead, have evidence for a power beyond us.

Further, while we are separating out a discussion of miracles from religious experience or mysticism, again we need to see the intimate connection between them and the way they mesh as evidence for God. Miracles often, but not always, are associated with the life and work of holy people who also may experience higher levels of the mystical life. And such higher states of the mystical life are themselves "miraculous" in some sense while also being continuous with the more normal prayer life of Christians.

One characteristic of a miracle, as understood as manifesting God's self-revelation, is that it is not simply a "freak event." If a rose suddenly appeared in midair and fell to the ground in the desert with no one around, it would hardly constitute the sort of miracle one finds described in the Bible or in lives of holy people. That is because such miracles are a matter of a communication of one self to other selves. They are meaningful communications such as those that occur in human language and words. As such they occur in contexts within which they make sense to those receiving them. As events that make sense they are evidence of the communication of another spiritual knowing and loving being.

In this way we can see C. S. Lewis was right in his discussion of miracles to argue that if the naturalist or reductionist philosopher were to try to deny them as impossible he would also have to deny free, human communication, and therefore his own communication. In terms of cognitional structure we can see that someone, the one denying that miracles can happen, has used his intelligence and reason to work out his argument and has chosen to communicate this to us for a reason. But he is denying that anyone can do all this because the laws of nature prevent it. We saw this kind of self-destructive reductionism earlier in the book, the kind that is seen in behaviorist denial of our freedom to act for a proposed end.

To deny as some like Hume have done that miracles can happen because it would be a break in the iron laws of nature is, then, to land oneself in this self-destructive denial of human intelligent and reasonable behavior and self-communication. It is also to show a massive naivety as regards the way science, through which we come to know of any putative laws, is dependent on human rationality, which only arrives, at best, at highly probable judgments about what there is in nature. Furthermore, the old determinist view on laws in nature has been replaced by the modern scientific worldview that holds laws in nature to be regularities that are more or less probable regarding their emergence and survival. They are not what *must* be. This, in its turn, is a further aspect of what we saw in the chapter on metaphysics regarding contingency. The "laws of nature" as described in the best theories of modern science are doubly contingent, we may say. As nonnecessary, in the sense that only God is necessary, their nonexistence can be thought because their "what" is contingent (does not have to be). And in addition they are contingent because their emergence and survival in the unfolding of the universe is only what might come about, not what has to come about. The miraculous cannot be ruled out a priori, then, no more than meaningful human communication can be ruled out "in the name of science" (of course that means not by science per se but by a particular philosophical view of science).

If we have reason to think that God, as a personal being, exists, we can be on the lookout to see how God may communicate with us (and as we said before the evidence also runs in the other direction: from evidence that God *has* communicated to the existence of God). What about assessing if and when this communication has occurred? What we would be looking for would be (a) instances of meaningful communication, (b) communication that would be about the Creator's will for the human created creature, (c) events and occurrences that are very difficult to explain away as anything but such communication. Of course (c) is the area that has to bear the burden of proof. In order to establish such an occurrence as probable we should use all the tests established by good reasoning in history, medicine, unbiased psychiatry, and sound human common sense. Of course we know of all kinds of fraud, trickery, delusion, legend, myth, psychosomatic disorders, and the like in human history and the history of religion.

We also have to consider the fact that apparent self-communication from God could possibly be communication from other spiritual entities such as evil spirits. So the discussion of miracles naturally opens up, in a philosophical way, to more general discussion of the paranormal, of ghosts, poltergeists, and evil spirits, and on such areas as evidence for life after death from near-death experiences and the like.

Anthony Flew spent much of his professional career as a philosopher writing against belief in God and religious faith. Late in life he has become a theist through his dialogues with the writer Roy Varghese. In an earlier book titled *The Logic of Mortality*, Flew tackled the question of life after death and looked at evidence of this from the paranormal: apparitions, near-death experiences, hauntings, poltergeists, and other phenomena. He admitted that once careful and critical research had cleared away cases of hysteria, fake, and legend, there were plenty of instances that could not be easily explained away. In the end he opted for the view that these things might be caused by forces within the person receiving the phenomena themselves, forces that would eventually be explained away by science.

While this can be granted in some cases there are many others that cannot be explained in this way. In careful research, conducted by groups such as the Society for Psychical Research, there are cases of poltergeist phenomena, apparitions, and hauntings that can no doubt be explained in this way. Some hauntings seem to be rather like some kind of emotional imprint of human experience that is then replayed like a "lifeless" recording to certain recipients. But many other cases of such events are unlike this. Many cases have all the hallmarks of there being an intelligent, intentional entity communicating with human recipients of the communication. So the person who experiences the encounter has no record before or after of being able to cause or bring about such phenomena; different persons, unknown to each other, experience similar phenomena in the same locations; these phenomena are not like a "dead tape recording" but manifest an "intelligent" responding to the different individuals in the different circumstances in which they witness the phenomena.

If, in the final analysis, we take an a priori view, as Flew does, that such varied data cannot be the manifestation of disembodied intelligent entities but must be explained away by a reductionist scientific account, then we are in immediate danger of hyperbolic doubt. What does that mean? Well, we are in a similar situation with regard to the thoughts and intentions of those around us; we do not directly experience their consciousness as we do our own. So we cannot rule out, say, that what someone says to us is not the result of some alien controlling them like a dummy or a machine. If we take the road of hyperbolic doubt (as we see in the case of Descartes' doubting all that can be doubted or the pathology of the archconspiracy theorists) then we end up in the unreasonable position of demanding certainty where we should be content with probable judgments. If we can reach probable judgments about the thoughts and wishes of those around us, we can use the same criteria to reason to the best explanation in the cases of certain "paranormal" situations—that it is an intentional, intelligent entity that is trying to communicate with us. If we take the option of saying, "Well, maybe it is the unconscious of the person themselves," we may end up by attributing such incredible powers to this person's unconscious (powers they perhaps have not manifested before the event in question and do not afterwards), including knowledge of all kinds of things not known to the person's consciousness, that our hypothesis is really not less radical than that of saying it is another intelligent entity doing the work; for this "unconscious" of the recipient ends up looking like another consciousness living within them.

In addition, we have to take into consideration what was said above about the interlocking of the moral and rational in this context. Just like the question of whether or not to risk digging down to see if the noise under the earthquake rubble is another survivor trying to communicate, so in the cases we have been discussing, we need to be aware that if there is evidence of a "miraculous" communication it may be important to try to respond appropriately, given some evidence that this is the case, but not, perhaps, overwhelming evidence. This may not be the kind of evidence we can have about some of our own conscious states (as we see in cognitional theory), but it may be, as analysis could show, not much different from the cases of the communications of the conscious intentions of those around us in ordinary life.

In fact the Catholic Church has for some centuries had very stringent processes of evaluation for supposed miracles, apparitions, and other such events. The Congregation for the Causes of Saints in the Vatican has exercised such oversight over centuries. Such procedures of the Catholic Church, which have involved the work of the famous devil's advocate, demonstrate the kind of reasoned assessment of the evidence we have been discussing. There is no a priori dismissing of all such cases due to philosophical prejudices that are themselves philosophically questionable, but, rather, there is a robust caution exercised such that what are deemed genuine cases of miracles and apparitions of, say, the Virgin Mary and other saints have to pass stringent tests. On the basis of such criteria and by employing this methodology, numerous cases of the miraculous and of apparitions have been assessed and judged credible.

## Mystical Experience

In their lengthy and detailed writings, the sixteenth-century Spanish mystics St. Teresa of Avila (d. 1582) and St. John of the Cross (d. 1591) express insights that are found throughout the mystical tradition of the church. In these writings we find a wealth of fine-grained psychological and spiritual analyses of the path followed by the Christian who finds himself or herself called to a particular mystical vocation. These writings explain in depth the stages of this journey from, perhaps, a period of enthusiasm through periods of aridity and what is known as the "dark night" to stages of ultimate, intimate union with God—a union that seems the highest attainable in this life for mere mortals. In these writings the fundamental criteria of authentic growth are shown to us: that "progress" is defined in terms of ever more mature human balance and a deepening commitment to love of God and love of others.

It is very difficult to dismiss, therefore, as hysteria or self-hypnosis the claims made about the highest states of mystical union with God that one finds in such writings and others like them. Rather, the writings themselves explain and warn about mere enthusiasm and ordinary psychological suggestion. John of the Cross explains, for instance, that "visions" may be from God or from the evil one or from our ordinary psychological processes. Rather, the highest mystical states of union have nothing to do with hysteria or even "apparently physical" images and visions.

The data experienced by the recipient in an apparition would be that of, say, the image of a person, their words, and the emotional and psychological reactions of the recipient. Thus one could misrepresent such an experience as being true to the reality it purports to show, as one does when one thinks a mirage is a true image of an oasis. And in assessing the genuineness of an apparition other criteria may need to be invoked: does the individual involved receive information that they could not have otherwise? Are there physical signs apparent to them and others? And (together with these) does the experience contribute to a genuine human growth in holiness? Nevertheless, in the case of the experience of the highest mystical union with God, described in detail in the writings of the mystics we have mentioned, the very data are not some images to be interpreted one way or another but the conscious experience of union with another consciousness, experienced to be the consciousness of the infinite, the absolute source of love and meaning, beyond the contingency and "poverty" of the recipient. The description of such union with God strikes home with any reader as an authentic account of an "encounter" with what every human mind and heart really desires: the infinite source of truth, meaning, love, and beauty.

It is perhaps no wonder then that it was through spending a night reading the works of St. Teresa of Avila that the brilliant Jewish philosopher Edith Stein, who up to that point was agnostic, was converted to the Catholic faith. Stein was the assistant to Edmund Husserl, the founding father of phenomenology, and no doubt her skill as a careful analyst of the various states—the emotive, intellectual, and interpersonal states—of human consciousness provided a good background for her conviction that what St. Teresa was writing was the truth. Another philosopher who was led to Catholicism through the writings of the great mystics was the philosopher of evolution Henri Bergson (d. 1941).

A point we can also make here is that in the writings of the great Catholic mystics (we have mentioned only two from among very many) we find all that we may also see in the great works of oriental mysticism concerning the expansion of consciousness, the experience of the absolute and the infinite, and so forth, but we also find much more. We also see that their experience is at once the experience of an infinite personal God, the triune God of Three Persons, who is the fullness of being, but at once an intimate lover of the soul.

## The Founder of Christianity

The argument for the reasonableness of opting for Christianity must, of course, rest in a fundamental way on the question of whether or not it is reasonable to believe the things that the Christian faith says about its founder, Jesus of Nazareth. But before we say something on this issue, we should also remind ourselves of the point about interlocking and mutually supportive evidence for a reasoned case that we have stressed here. So the evidence coming from the tradition of the church that there are cases of miracles and visions that, after passing stringent examination, it is reasonable to believe is also evidence that links with the historical claims that such things occurred in the life of Christ. There are cases of the multiplication of food due to the prayers of a holy person, in the life of the nineteenth-century St. John Vianney (d. 1859), for example, that have passed the strict tests of authenticity applied by church authorities. The strictly controlled area of the church's involvement in exorcisms (which has for a good many years involved the cooperation of psychiatrists) also witnesses to cases of demonic activity that are really difficult to explain away in other terms. Thus these later historical cases interlock as evidence for authenticity when we read about similar cases in the life of Christ. Indeed, those in the tradition of the church claim that it is precisely through the power of Christ that these later miracles and exorcism occur. We have here, then, a case of what philosophers call a "hermeneutical circle": the present helps us interpret past events and vice versa.

Our point about interlocking evidence goes further: if there is reason to believe in a personal God, then there is reason to think this God may communicate to us how we should reach that fulfillment, the desire for which has been created in our nature. Such fulfillment, such reaching God, will be in the context of a world that is marked by human moral failure and by evil. So we are on the lookout as we survey human history for God's answer to us and the solution to the evil that so thwarts human goodness. We would expect then that God's answer in history will be an unambiguous and coherent answer that reaches to human persons across time and space. If there is the evidence of holy, integrated lives, and these lives are seen as emerging from a certain tradition, and such lives and the tradition are marked also by miraculous events, such that there is evidence that these witness to a communication from God, then already we may be disposed to sympathetically examine the claims made for the origins of this essentially coherent tradition (albeit still, unfortunately, marked by human failure and sin on the part of those who do not respond to the resources offered) in the life, teachings, and work of its founder.

The philosophical area known as hermeneutics is, in fact, crucial when we approach the question of the historicity of the life of Christ as this is portrayed in the gospels, the other writings of the New Testament, and in early church traditions.

The media and popular press occasionally seem to attack the life of Christ from the viewpoint of sensationalistic stories debunking the gospel accounts. All this points to the importance of a university education. What I mean is that such "popular" stories and news items rarely give the impression that there is, in fact, a whole academic industry in the universities of the world that deals with biblical research and questions such as the historicity of the gospels, and there has been for nearly two centuries. What one may see occasionally in such television programs is some academic chosen because he or she represents something of an extreme viewpoint. But very rarely is the public treated to a proper debate with serious academic New Testament scholars involved: that would hardly be sensationalistic enough. One is reminded of the old *Monty Python* spoof on such "shock! horror!" debunking stories: in one of their shows we were treated to the sensationalistic documentary *Was God a Dinosaur?*

One needs, then, to turn to the work of internationally recognized scholars in the area of studies on the historical Jesus if one wants sound evidence for the fundamental reliability of the gospels on the life of Christ. One can mention here such first-rate academics as N. T. Wright, Ben Meyer (d. 1995), and Rainer Riesner, among many others, and these built, in turn, on the massive scholarship of previous generations that witnessed great scholars such as Joachim Jeremias (d. 1979), C. H. Dodd (d. 1973), and Pierre Benoit (d. 1987). One recent work that should be recommended here is John Redford's *Bad, Mad or God.* This is a superb work of apologetics in the best sense: apologetics should be giving a reason for the faith one holds, not a matter of cheap rhetoric. Redford is not only an expert biblical scholar but also has the ability of bringing to bear vast knowledge in the field on the type of questions people naturally and reasonably ask: Did Jesus exist? Was he like the gospels say he was? Did he work miracles? Was there a resurrection? Was there a virgin birth? Redford brings his scholarship to bear in answering each of these questions step by step. Thus he shows we have abundant evidence for the existence of Jesus (from the interlocking evidence of biblical sources and extrabiblical sources, both pagan and Christian) and for the fundamental reliability of the gospels' accounts of his life, teaching, miracles, and resurrection. The evidence makes highly probable, then, our estimation of the fundamental literary genre of the gospels as being that of truly telling us about the life of the founder of Christianity. Naturally, these are not meant to be camcorder accounts. But the tradition of the church from St. Augustine on was that the gospel writers selected from the material that came to them according to theological interests and that they did not always give us verbatim the words of Christ but sometimes gave, rather, the sense of his teaching and message. In this we can say they were not very different from modern historians writing the biographies of world figures such as Churchill or Stalin.

Redford, however, like other scholars in the field, including some we have mentioned, is well aware of the hermeneutical problems. By this we mean that interpreting documents of the past involves our present outlook. The issue of the miraculous comes up again. If, as has happened with various scholars, we have the a priori view that miracles don't happen, then naturally we will explain away all the putative events in the New Testament in the same way as we saw a philosopher like Flew doing with any such putative events in our own time. So the historian has to be aware of this hermeneutical circle. Redford brilliantly reveals what happens in certain traditions of interpretation since the Enlightenment once one has assumed, uncritically we would argue, the a priori view that miracles *can't* happen. If this is so then it may very well be a case of refusing to let one's view be challenged either by philosophical arguments to the contrary or by the evidence that comes both from the past and from the present.

## Opting for a Religion

One of the objections raised when people are discussing miracles and mystical phenomena is that when one looks across the religions of the world there are such phenomena aplenty and they therefore contradict each other, since they emerge from divergent and opposed religions.

The question about an apparent multiplicity of religious claims is a very important one: if we have reason to believe, from arguments, that there is a personal God, and if we are on the lookout for that God in our lives and in history, then we should expect that God to offer a coherent, not contradictory, answer to our questions about how to live, how to find and follow God's will. A contradictory answer to such questions would be no answer at all.

Therefore, the question itself suggests an important criterion for discerning a possible case of God's self-revelation in history. It would be an answer that would be coherent. That is, it would be an answer that spread across human history in time and space, that remained unified and within which the various signs of God's self-manifestation cohered in a continuity in truth. The teaching and the genuine signs, miracles, mystical phenomena, and holiness of those who lived up to the resources of the tradition would all cohere.

Other criteria that we might invoke in trying to discern the central and coherent revelation of God amid all the various religious phenomena that exist in history could be drawn from philosophical resources such as those already outlined and argued for in this book. So we could ask if a given religious tradition was really wide of the mark when it came to certain ethical and metaphysical positions regarding human persons, God, and the universe.

Thus with regard to Christianity one can find interlocking arguments from the existence of God, miracles, and mystical experience both that a personal God exists and that this God is revealed in history. So in arguing for the existence of God it was argued that the ultimate explanation of contingent reality would also need to be the exemplary cause and the final cause. As such, if that explanation does not have anything like intelligence and will, then it is no explanation, for an insufficient explanation is no explanation at all when we are dealing with the principle of the intelligibility of being (a principle that we cannot coherently deny). This argument for a personal God, then, coheres with the mystical experience of the great Christian mystics, and it coheres with the cases of the miraculous (that have been carefully investigated), since these are experienced as manifesting an "Other" who is an intelligent and loving being (as perhaps confirming a teaching and/or answering prayers). Above all it coheres with the holiness of life, teaching, miracles, and resurrection of the founder of Christianity, Jesus of Nazareth, whose life can be historically authenticated through sound, modern, historical scholarship.

On the other hand one would have to begin, in looking at other world religions, by noting that as regards modern scholarship there would be no question that certain key religious figures, purported to have lived thousands of years ago, cannot be seen as anything but mythical, or at best we have tiny fragments of reliable historical information about them. Further, when we turn to the question of the paranormal and miracles, certain religious cultures have not shared the same concerns with the interrelationship between faith and reason as has been evident in the history of Christianity, and so one has not witnessed attempts to sift out legends and cases of popular myth as one has in, say, the work of the body in the Catholic Church concerned with alleged miracles in the lives of holy people.

One then has to say that paranormal phenomena coming from the various religious traditions of the world may indeed manifest the spiritual nature of the human person, in the sense that the spiritual powers that we possess may manifest themselves more clearly in states of meditation and other exercises. In addition we should also say that, as it was suggested above, there is evidence from the Christian tradition of exorcism of the existence of evil spirits at work in human lives and history.

It is important to point to all these different aspects of possible spiritual activity when one is responding to the person who asks about the diversity of phenomena across religions. Some Christians have, in fact, claimed that all genuine miraculous manifestations in non-Christian religions have been the work of evil spirits. But this has not been the line taken by all. Pope Benedict XIV (1740–58), in his work *On Canonization*, follows St. Thomas Aquinas in saying that examples of miraculous intervention by God in response to pagan prayers may be genuine: they demonstrate God's providential love for all creation and people. Further, as we said above, paranormal occurrences in various religions may be the manifestation of "natural" powers that we have as spiritual beings. What I think theologians who follow the line taken by Pope Benedict and St. Thomas might say is that such instances of miraculous intervention by God will not coalesce in history in such a way as to send out a confused and contradictory message about where God's definitive answer is to be found in human history. Rather they will, in their expression of God's personal and providential care for all people, point toward a religious tradition in which God's self-revelation is most coherently and definitely manifest.

It should perhaps be emphasized at this point that I am not trying to "knock" the great religions of the world other than Christianity. Of course I would want to acknowledge all that is great, good, and noble in the various religious traditions of the world, traditions that point toward a more authentic vision of human life and reality than that seen in Western materialism. As one can see from the words addressed by Pope Pius XII to the meeting of bishops in Mumbai in 1950 or, more fully, in the teaching *Nostra Aetate* of the Second Vatican Council, the Catholic Church recognizes all that is truly good, noble, and spiritual in the world religions and sees the Holy Spirit at work in them. At the same time the church teaches that only in the unique incarnation in Jesus Christ is the definitive fullness of salvation found, and, also, there are negative and ambiguous elements present in the nature of other world religions. I would subscribe entirely to that viewpoint.

What we are concerned with here, however, is the perspective of the philosophy of religion. We have seen earlier in this book how philosophy should help to move one beyond the sometimes simplistic and contradictory viewpoints in modern Western culture. It is a very good thing that religious bigotry and violence have been rejected in the West. But it is not helpful to replace them with self-contradictory notions of religious truth. What we should respect and treasure is the human person who puts forth views, even if we disagree with those views. In the present discussion we are concerned with establishing whether or not there is anything good or true in any religious viewpoint, and we have been arguing against the view that there is nothing true or good in any of them. This does not mean that we want to insult or denigrate the atheist with whom we disagree. On the contrary we want him or her to come to share in a fuller, more joyous vision of reality. But if this has been the line taken, then it is only honest to continue it and ask if there is anything that commends one religion more than another. The view that all religions are equally valid, just like the view that they are all equally false and, perhaps, evil, needs to be argued for; from the philosophical viewpoint it cannot be just assumed.

It has been argued that the religious phenomena evident in Christianity cohere with a philosophical position that argues for a personal God. The Christian worldview also coheres with the philosophical position on ethics and the human person argued for in this book. In the pillars of Scripture, tradition, and magisterium (teaching authority of the church) on which Catholic Christianity is founded one sees the means by which God could secure agreement and continuity in truth between peoples across times, places, and cultures. In this way the divine answer of God's self-sacrificial love can touch and transform the peoples of the world, whose very nature it is to seek ultimate answers to the ultimate questions that we human beings raise.

# Concluding Remarks

The journey we have made in this book is one of self-discovery. It has been one in which you have been encouraged to use your intelligence and reason to come to know in a more explicit and detailed way key features of that very intelligence and reason. Because that is not a matter of closing you off in some subjective, false dreamworld, but rather a matter of coming to know an aspect of reality, of being, that is the reality of yourself, our discussion then opened up to metaphysics, which is philosophical knowledge of basic features and structures of reality. We then went on to look at the area of ethics and showed how the approach of verifying positions in your own conscious reality can help in deciding for or against certain basic views current in philosophy on what is good or bad, right or wrong. In the final chapter the discussion was extended into the area of the philosophy of religion. The implications of some of the key aspects argued for in metaphysics (especially intelligibility) were seen to lead to an affirmation of the existence of God. We then asked whether we could also apply criteria of intelligence, reason, and moral choosing to the question of whether or not one should opt for the Christian religion.

All along the approach has been one of asking you to check out the fundamental positions argued for in your own conscious experience of yourself. As intimate and personal as that process is, it comes about only through dialogue with others. This dialogue could not begin without the formation given to us by our family and cultural tradition in which we have been brought up, provided with a language and a background of ideas, skills, and values to start from. I hope that you will continue the journey of self-discovery through futher dialogue with the great philosophical tradition. Since the approach taken in this book is fundametally that of Bernard Lonergan, I hope you will continue the journey of self-discovery through reading his work and also discovering the great tradition that he appropriates, makes his own, in his writings. That is the tradition of Aristotle, St. Augustine, St. Thomas Aquinas, and John Henry Newman, a tradition that Lonergan appropriates in the light of, and in critical dialogue with, modern philosophy, science, mathematics, and scholarship. In order to help you on that continued journey I have placed a list of suggested further reading at the end of this book.

# Suggested Further Reading

\* indicates a beginner's level book; ** indicates intermediate level; ***
indicates advanced

** Beards, Andrew. *Objectivity and Historical Understanding*. Aldershot: Ashgate,
    1997.
*** ———. *Method in Metaphysics: Lonergan and the Future of Analytical Phi-
    losophy*. Toronto: University of Toronto Press, 2008.
\* Chesterton, G. K. *Orthodoxy*. Rockville, MD: Serenity Publishers, 2008.
\* Crean, Thomas. *God Is No Delusion: A Refutation of Richard Dawkins*. San
    Francisco: Ignatius Press, 2007.
\* Davies, Brian. *An Introduction to the Philosophy of Religion*. Oxford: Oxford
    University Press, 2004.
** ———. *The Thought of Thomas Aquinas*. Oxford: Clarendon Press, 1993.
\* Egan, Philip. *Philosophy and Catholic Theology: A Primer*. Collegeville, MN:
    Liturgical Press, 2009.
\* Flanagan, Joseph. *Quest for Self-Knowledge*. Toronto: University of Toronto
    Press, 1997.
** Fitzpatrick, Joseph. *Philosophical Encounters: Lonergan and the Analytic Tradi-
    tion*. Toronto: University of Toronto Press, 2005.
\* Gaarder, Jostein. *Sophie's World*. London: Orion Books, 1994.
\* Haldane, John. *An Intelligent Person's Guide to Religion*. London: Gerald Duck-
    worth and Co. Ltd., 2005.
** Jaki, Stanley. *Science and Creation*. Edinburgh: Scottish Academic Press,
    1986.
** ———. *God and the Cosmologists*. Edinburgh: Scottish Academic Press,
    1989.
\* Kreeft, Peter. *A Short Summa*. San Francisco: Ignatius Press, 1993.
** Liddy, Richard. *Startling Strangeness*. University Press of America, 2006.

\*\*\* Lonergan, Bernard. *Insight: A Study of Human Understanding*. Edited by F. E. Crowe, R. M. Doran, and T. V. Daly. Toronto: University of Toronto Press, 1992.

\*\* ———. *Understanding and Being*. Edited by E. A. Morelli, M. Morelli, F. E. Crowe, R. M. Doran, and T. V. Daly. Toronto: University of Toronto Press, 1990.

\*\*\* McCarthy, Michael. *The Crisis of Philosophy*. New York: SUNY Press, 1990.

\*\* Meynell, Hugo. *Redirecting Philosophy*. Toronto: University of Toronto Press, 1998.

\*\* ———. *Postmodernism and the New Enlightenment*. Washington, DC: The Catholic University of America Press, 1999.

\*\* Morelli, Mark D., and Elizabeth A. Morelli, eds. *The Lonergan Reader*. Toronto: University of Toronto Press, 1997.

\* Nagel, Thomas. *What Does It All Mean? A Very Short Introduction to Philosophy*. Oxford: Oxford University Press, 1987.

\* Osborne, Richard. *Philosophy for Beginners*. New York: Writers and Readers Publishing, 1992.

\* Pope John Paul II. *Fides et Ratio* (On Faith and Reason). London: CTS, 1998.

\* Pope Benedict XVI. *Truth and Tolerance*. Translated by Henry Taylor. San Francisco: Ignatius Press, 2004.

\* Redford, John. *Bad, Mad or God? Proving the Divinity of Christ from St. John's Gospel*. London: St. Paul's Press, 2004.

\* Tekippe, Terry. *What Is Lonergan Up to in* Insight*? A Primer*. Collegeville, MN: Liturgical Press, 1996.

\*\* Varghese, Roy, ed. *Theos, Anthropos, Christos: A Compendium of Modern Philosophical Theology*. New York: Peter Lang, 2000.

\* Vitz, Paul. *Faith of the Fatherless: The Psychology of Atheism*. Dallas, TX: Spence Publishing Company, 2009.

# Index